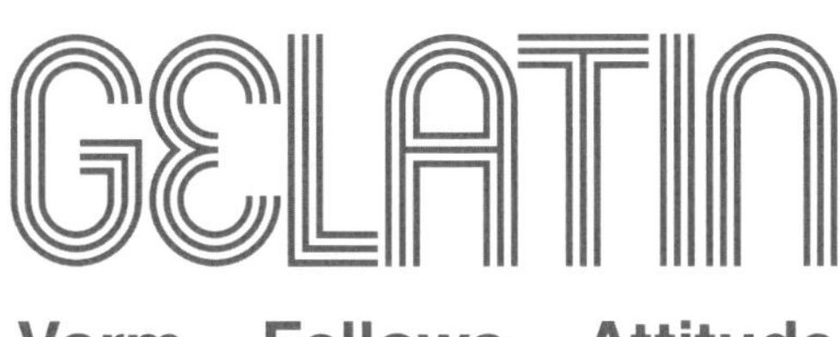

GELATIN

Vorm – Fellows – Attitude

museum van
boijmans beuningen   Verlag der Buchhandlung Walther König

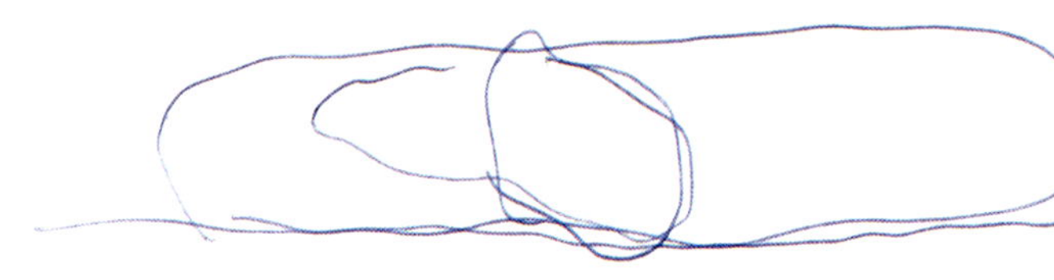

Sjarel Ex
Director
Museum Boijmans Van Beuningen

With a population of 635,000, we speak 176 languages in this metropolis on the North Sea. The city of Rotterdam and countless private individuals, patrons and collectors have been supporting their art museum for almost 170 years now. Museum Boijmans Van Beuningen hosts a collection of magnificent works—beginning with Bosch and Bruegel—and oversees six centuries of art and design history. Year in and year out, major exhibitions and shows, focusing on our collection, link the city, a world port, with its visitors and art.

Our permanent collection is never static; we add to it all the time and create new insights and configurations. The collection reads like a mirror of art history and society, old and new, always in motion, international in its make-up, a continual source of conversation and discussion. Shows at Museum Boijmans Van Beuningen are seen by the keen and young, the experienced and curious. Our visitors are local, national and international. In the tradition of Erasmus, we seek dialogue in the bubbling international

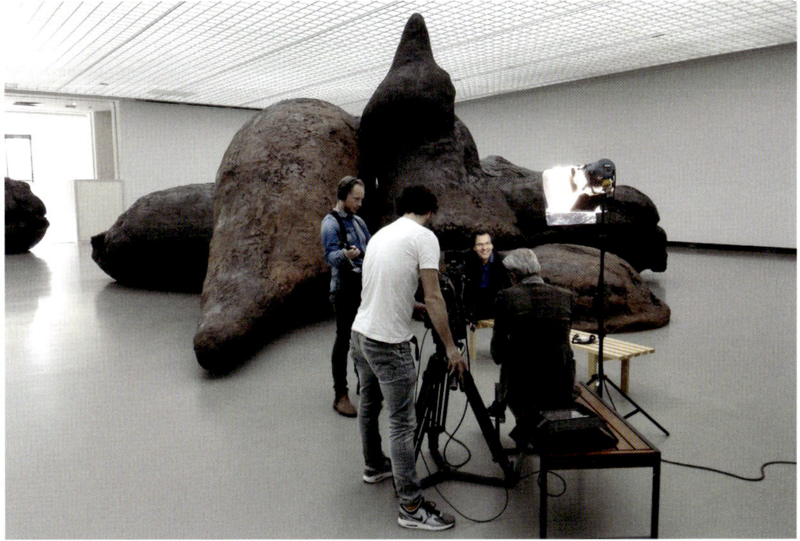

context in which the museum sits.

Making an exhibition with Gelatin is a challenge and a highpoint. Convinced of one another's freethinking attitudes and standards and with great confidence on both sides, we created an exhibition in the tradition of previous experimental installations shown in our galleries. The Museum Boijmans Van Beuningen's program, in which Walter de Maria, Harald Szeeman, Olafur Eliasson, Ernesto Neto, Carsten Höller, Urs Fischer and many others excelled, has been enriched by four extraordinary sculptures, designed and assembled for the site by Gelatin, along with 101 gender-neutral, or should I say gender-neutralizing, nude suits.

From the exhibition's opening, thousands of people, including the international press, embraced and condemned it with equal enthusiasm. Personally, I'll never forget how, on a quiet Tuesday morning, a group of four American girls, smartphones at the ready, watched as one of them hauled herself into a suit featuring the largest possible dick achievable with a sewing machine (we learned not to be mealy-mouthed during the exhibition). As she wandered around, to the great hilarity of her friends, she crowed: "I've got him, finally!" It was just one of the many times when, as a participant standing back, looking and evaluating, I thought that visual impressions and experiences had been created that even surpassed Jheronymus Bosch's work. I would like to thank Gelatin and the sponsors, and of course my team, for making this excellent exhibition possible.

**GELATIN IN CONVERSATION
WITH SCOTT CLIFFORD EVANS**
Gelatin Studio Vienna,
June 2018

I. MOTHERS, SHIT, ETERNITY, AND DEATH

Have your mothers seen images of these sculptures and what have they said about them?

Ali: I will show it to my mother the next time I see her.

Wolfgang: My mother hasn't seen it yet, but she saw images of the exhibition because she is on our email newsletter. But the last time I was at my countryside home, some neighbors had a party out of their wine cellar. I went there and they asked me where I have been for so long. I told them I was in Rotterdam and showed them some images and they were very, very impressed.

Scott: Really…

Wolfgang: Because finally they understand what I am doing.

Ali: Because they are doing it too.

Tobias: My mother saw a guy shitting my fist.

Ali: Shit into your fist?

Tobias: Shitting my fist.

Ali: Shitting your fist?

Tobias: Yeah, my fist was in his…

Ali: But that's not shit, that's your fist. That's something else.

Tobias: You have to have shit in the process of getting something out of your anus?

Scott: He was shitting out your fist.

Ali: Yeah, but that's not shitting because not everything that comes out of…

Tobias: But it's shitting.

Ali: It's a sensation of shitting, but it's not shit. There's a difference.

Wolfgang: Is that shitting? I didn't know.

Tobias: Sure, I mean, when it comes out of his ass, he shits it.

Ali: Yeah, but it's not shit.

Wolfgang: Not everything that comes out of your anus is shit.

Tobias: But it *smelled* like shit.

Scott: So when a penis comes out of an ass is the ass shitting the penis out?

Ali: That's an interesting question because the feeling of shitting… I spend a lot of time on the toilet because it just feels so nice to shit. So of course you can make this feeling better by enhancing it, but the programming of the sphincter through society and culture and so on is really strong. So it's nice to play around these boundaries.

Wolfgang: But there's also not really that big of a difference between shitting and speaking.

Ali: Do you know the story of the talking asshole?

Scott: Like in William S. Burroughs?

Ali: Yeah, it's somebody whose asshole starts speaking and then

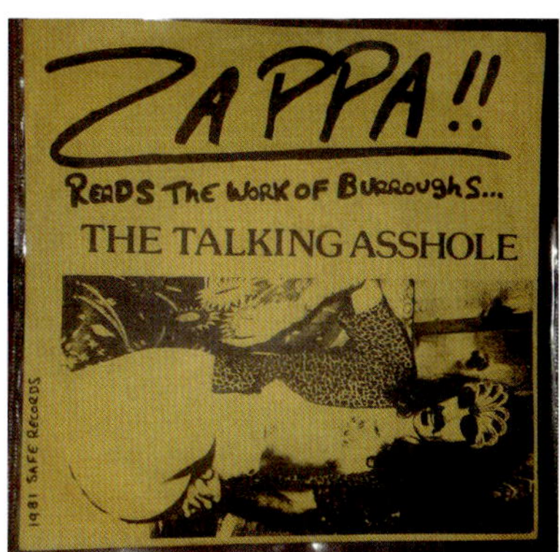

Zappa, *The Talking Asshole,* 7" vinyl, 1981

the speaking asshole gets more and more dominance in his life. His head starts shriveling down. Then all of a sudden he starts walking on his hands and his asshole becomes his main form of expression, "excretion." Did you know that the origin for the words "secret" and "secretion" is the same?

Wolfgang: But I would not say that everything that comes out of the ass is shit.

Tobias: Is shit a secretion?

Wolfgang: What about a fart? When air comes out of the ass it's not shit, it's fart.

Ali: And sometimes the ass can inhale. If you're really trained, you can make it do the opposite, you know, something goes in and up and up and up and up…

Tobias: Inverted shitting…

Ali: That's when you make the mouth into the asshole…

Tobias: …and then you burp?

Wolfgang: But Tobias is German,

probably everything is shit to him.

Tobias: But if you suck in the air from the ass can you burp better? Can you press the air up your stomach?

Ali: There are so many muscles in between, not just sphincter. First, there's the big chamber, you know, where the shit goes to dry, like a storage space. Then to the side there's the sigmoid. It comes off of the big intestine. The sigmoid starts with a lot of rings of contraction and they are made by how your body works to transport things forward and out. So you have a lot of nerves in the stomach. It's like a little brain. And the coordination of all these muscles to pump something through and check if it is the right consistency, and flavor, is very complex. So to train your brain to take something in the other direction is possible but really challenging because you have to learn a new way to access your ass.

Tobias: When I had my fist in that ass, I didn't feel all these muscles.

Ali: Because that guy was wide.

Tobias: But these muscles you cannot control by your mind, by your will.

Ali: You can. You can learn to control everything with your mind.

Scott: Florian, has your mother seen images of the exhibition

and what has she said about it?

Florian: No. No, I don't think so. How would she have?

Tobias: I sent my mother images. Let me see what she answered…

Scott: Did you send her a link to an article?

Florian: She doesn't have a computer. My mother doesn't "link."

Wolfgang: But it was in the daily Austrian newspapers…

Florian: Maybe she has seen it. I'm not sure.

Tobias: It looks like my mother hasn't answered anything.

Wolfgang: I sent my mother images and she doesn't answer either.

Ali: My mother asked for images, but I didn't show her yet because I didn't have time.

Wolfgang: What were you so busy doing?

Ali: I was eating and then falling asleep and then leaving again.

Tobias: See [shows the message on his phone] she doesn't answer.

Wolfgang: What is she supposed to say?

Tobias: "Great show."

Ali: No, "great shit."

Tobias: Usually my mother says "I'm so happy for you." That's what mothers usually answer, no?

Scott: Because who sees your shit first? Your mother sees your shit first, right?

Ali: It depends on who's looking at your shit first.

Tobias: Elsa and Leo both, the first thing that they did when they were born, other than breathing, when laying on the belly, was taking a shit...on their feet.

Wolfgang: But isn't shouting the first thing babies do?

Tobias: Sure, you come out and then start breathing and then...

Wolfgang: ...because this is also important. I talked to a person and he told me that shitting is the first thing, but I thought it's the crying, the shouting.

Ali: I think the breathing is first.

Wolfgang: Actually, "the word" comes before shit.

Tobias: Yeah, shit is when you start relaxing: relaxed, on the belly, ten minutes after birth, they both took a shit.

What do you see as the relationship between shit and death?

Florian: Shit is *life.*

Ali: Death is too.

Florian: Maybe the relationship is...

Ali: "Relation*shit*"

Florian: You have to die...and you have to shit.

Ali: I see it differently.

Florian: There're not many things you *really* have to do.

Tobias: Breathe, die, shit.

Ali: The relationshit is...

Florian: You don't have to breathe...you just die.

Wolfgang: But we don't really work on the concept of death. It's not really around us.

Ali: It goes through me everyday.

Wolfgang: Sure, you have your depression every Sunday and you die every Saturday...

Ali: No! Every shit every second! It's a normal thing in life.

Wolfgang: But not in our work.

Tobias: How long does it take, if you don't shit, until you die?

Ali: I think about death every second.

Wolfgang: But not when you work.

Ali: Sure!

Florian: One of the girls who came to Rotterdam to see the show said that when she was a child and was shitting she was always super worried, she cried, because she lost a part of her body. It belongs to her and now it's gone. Somebody takes it away and flushes it, but it's a part of her body. I had never heard that before.

Wolfgang: We are more interested in eternity than death.

Ali: But death is part of eternity, no?

Wolfgang: Come on Ali, don't be so...

Ali: But what you're talking about is exactly that.

Wolfgang: But I don't believe in the concept of death where you go to heaven or hell or there's some...

Ali: You just disappear and then something else happens...that's eternity.

Florian: You disintegrate.

Wolfgang: Eternity is a different concept.

Ali: Why?

Tobias: There's eternity?

Ali: It happens again and again.

Wolfgang: It's a concept where you aren't important anymore, but people recall what you did.

Tobias: But there is eternity?

Wolfgang: Sure, you still listen to Mozart; you look at Leonardo da Vinci.

Tobias: Eternity is forever.

Wolfgang: Yeah, but who...ok, contemporary eternity...

Tobias: Then what's history?

Wolfgang: What's forever?

Tobias: Nothing.

Ali: Everything becomes shit. Everything becomes the same.

"Everything becomes shit. Everything becomes the same." Would you say that's your "philosophy of shit"?

Ali: Shit is way too positive because something grows out of it. And our shit sculptures are actually very nice compared to real shit.

Scott: Lately, random people have been shitting in front of my house in Vienna. Are you afraid this exhibition will inspire a trend of people shitting in public? On the streets of Rotterdam, for example?

Ali: We hope so because it's a way of expression that should be made visible in public again.

Florian: I was in India in 1991 or so and had never seen so much human shit on the street in my life. The beaches were also *full* of human excrement. The villages didn't have toilets. People went to the beach and took a shit on the beach.

Ali: That's gonna be the new summer holiday. You book a super fancy journey to the Seychelles and everybody just shits on the beach.

Florian: No, in India it was the beach of the village. People don't go to the beach to sunbathe or take a swim. They take a shit and the tide takes it away. But for 100 meters it was like "one here"

and "one here" and "one here," a meter apart.

Wolfgang: Was there toilet paper?

Florian: No.

Wolfgang: Because they wash in the sea.

Florian: I even had an encounter… In India, you walk down the street and see people crouching in a corner and taking a shit. I even walked by… There was this guy taking a shit and he says "Hello, hello! Mister, where you from?" and then he stops and his ass goes "pfft" and then he says, "Where you from? I speak English." He starts a conversation while he is taking a shit.

Tobias: But no shit was on top of another shit?

Florian: No.

The ancient Chinese had this practice of examining their shit to see how healthy it was.

Wolfgang: Really?

Scott: Yeah, totally.

Ali: It's also a European tradition.

Scott: So, every sculpture in the exhibition seems pretty well formed. How did you choose the forms and why was their no…

Wolfgang: Unhealthy one?

Scott: Yeah, why no diarrhea?

Wolfgang: It's sculpturally not so interesting.

Ali: Um-hum…

Wolfgang: Because it was an idea not to look over it.

Tobias: The same reason why there are not so many drawings of a plate of spaghetti.

Ali: Because it doesn't look good.

Tobias: That doesn't look good.

Scott: Well, the *Schlammsaal* (2006) at Kunsthaus Bregenz almost looks…it's very dirty and looks almost like diarrhea, very dirty, very messy.

Wolfgang: Then it's probably because we did it already.

Florian: But usually diarrhea is light and *Schlammsaal* was very black.

Ali: The shit from when you have diarrhea comes from far up your intestines. It smells different and it is much darker, like Flo says, it's black.

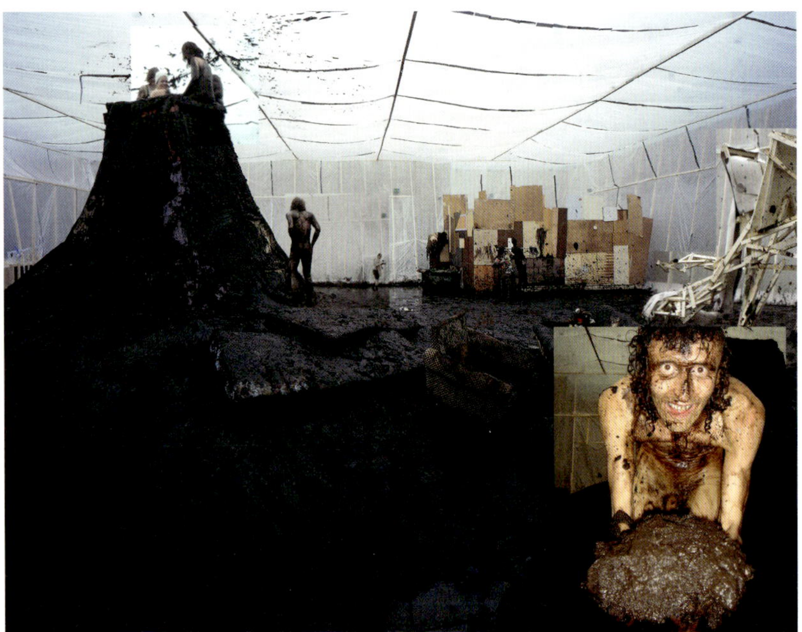

Schlammsaal, »Chinese Synthese Leberkäse«, Kunsthaus Bregenz, Austria, 2006

Florian: The diarrhea? No, it's light, not black.

Ali: It can be really black if it comes from really up.

Florian: Ok!

Tobias: I never had black diarrhea.

Wolfgang: I think then you probably have a kidney problem or something.

Scott: But I am curious, is this a difference in practice? If you compare *Schlammsaal* to the exhibition in Rotterdam, the Boijmans exhibition is quite clean.

Ali: Um-hum, it's very different because it's not about shit, it's about giving form. And which common form you can…how to make a nice sculpture, a nice form.

Wolfgang: Probably without *Schlammsaal* there wouldn't be Rotterdam. Maybe Rotterdam would be more diarrhea.

Ali: You have some liquid, mushy stuff and then your intestines prepare and dry it and then your sphincter makes the final articulation of how it's going to be on the plate or the toilet or wherever. So it's really a process of forming, being really sculptural with your body.

Why sculpt massive shits? Why the change in scale?

Wolfgang: Why not?

Ali: When you make art it's also about the artificial, to bring a certain point out, in a way. So if

you make it bigger you change the perspective and feeling in relation to it.

Wolfgang: Is it about the size?

Ali: You feel…you perceive it differently because all of a sudden you don't look down on it: you're *in* it. And you look up to it. You change your perspective and it becomes monumental. You can see and experience it differently. Anyway, the shits we made didn't smell. It was really about sculpture and form.

Wolfgang: The size is super natural. It wouldn't make sense any smaller. This is clear.

Ali: We decided they should be bigger so you cannot look over them.

Scott: You could have made a hundred small sculptures of shits…

Wolfgang: Yeah, but it's less interesting.

Scott: Why?

Wolfgang: It's not interesting, sculpturally, to do life-sized shit because everybody can do that much better than us. Everybody is doing it at least once a day.

Florian: I really like to take *big* shits. So when I need to shit, I wait. I wait for an hour, two hours, because I really want to take a big shit. I don't want to go to a toilet and make a "pffttt…" small thing…

Ali: Or if you want to have shit

sex with somebody you have to save up.

Florian: ...I really like to sit down and...

Ali: You never dreamt about taking a shit so big you could go inside it?

Wolfgang: Sure, I dreamt about it.

Ali: So you need a certain size so you can go inside it. That's a reason.

Wolfgang: For me the show is not about shit. It's not about big shit. Yeah, I dreamt a lot about entering my big shit or whatever... these walls of shit, but this is not what the exhibition is about.

Scott: What is it about?

Wolfgang: It's about the audience and the artist and what's in between.

How did you come to the form?

Wolfgang: There's one "iconic" shit, one "ironic" shit, one "family" shit and there's one "painful" shit. We tried to cover everything.

Scott: Which one's the painful shit?

Wolfgang: The one you see when you first enter.

Tobias: There's the idea of a form and then you try to sculpt a form. We didn't try to copy things we did in the toilet. The idea was not to make a realistic shit. A sphincter forms something that comes out, then you have this thing. You try to make it in a way that when you stand in front of this thing, you think, "This is a really good sculpture."

Ali: You study shit for all of your life and then you try to boil the essence out of it and you work on the "ultimate shit."

Wolfgang: All four sculptures in the show look like...when you see it, it immediately looks like shit, but none of these sculptures were ever shat before.

Tobias: Could be.

Wolfgang: No.

Tobias: You don't know.

Wolfgang: No. It's not about...

Tobias: ...It's not about if it's been shat before.

Wolfgang: But it's not about copying your shit.

Tobias: But it's also not important if this exact thing has been shat before.

Wolfgang: I think it's important.

Florian: The really great thing about working together, and Gelatin, is the schizophrenic quality that every single one of us can explain this show in a completely opposite and different way. And when you choose a topic or the content for a show and then you come to "shit" you realize that it's so simple and the simplicity of this shit makes it so complex that the schizophrenic machine starts working. Ali has a completely different approach towards shit than me. Wolfgang has an opposite approach to the content and topic of the show than Tobias. It's completely different, but you reduce it to a very, very primitive subject and form that gives room for a lot of associations.

Ali: It's the lowest common denominator.

Wolfgang: Maybe it's the highest.

Florian: You can associate with every level of society: personal, historical...

Wolfgang: I was also interested to "shit" inside a museum without making a joke out of it. This was challenging as well, for me. Not for Tobias maybe, or Ali, or Florian...

Ali: For me it was important to make it beautiful.

Wolfgang: It was important to do it without making a joke about it.

Tobias: That was important to you?

Wolfgang: Yeah.

Ali: That was important for me too.

Tobias: Why shouldn't it be a joke?

Ali: You could see it as a joke.

Florian: But we never do that.

Ali: Yeah, that's what we don't do in general.

Wolfgang: Exactly.

Tobias: But that's one small layer of interpretation—a very small, uninteresting layer.

Ali: Yeah.

Wolfgang: The size is a sculptural decision. Why is Michelangelo's *David* as big as it is, the size that it is? Every artwork has a size, yeah?

Florian: It's also about the artists' superego in their mid-life crises. They want to show the world that their shit is bigger than yours.

Ali: The sculptures are really a nice conversation piece because everybody can relate to them.

Tobias: Everybody has shit stories.

Wolfgang: Ali is right. And it was a content and form we could agree on.

Scott: Shit is a theme that comes up often in your work…

Tobias: …it relates very much to the body.

Scott: But shit itself was the actual material and now you use a different material to make shit.

Ali: Now we are really into "high" art, so we have gotten really artificial. It's more like rococo, actually we are less realistic than we used to be. Now it's really an artifice.

What's the importance of the rugs? Why shit on the rug?

Ali: Because you need a nice pedestal. It makes a difference if you shit on the street or in the toilet or on a rug.

Tobias: It gives it a meaning, a purpose. Like if you shit on the street, it's an accident. If you shit on a beautiful carpet, it's a purpose.

Ali: Like a statement.

Florian: Imagine somebody comes to your house and shits on your floor or shits on your carpet…

Ali: …or on your bed or on your pillow or on your face. It's all different.

Wolfgang: I think on the carpet it just looks shittier.

Tobias: No, it doesn't look shittier.

Ali: It just makes the shit look more beautiful, and the carpet as well.

Tobias: The carpet definitely becomes more beautiful.

Wolfgang: It's a decision.

Tobias: Exactly, it's a decision. If you do it on a carpet, it's a decision.

Ali: The Victoria and Albert Museum in London have the most famous Persian rug. It is lit for three minutes every hour in this huge glass box. It slowly lights up and you see this huge carpet with this really low ceiling where the lights are on. It's just the perfect place to put something on top. A carpet is *made* to put something on top.

Wolfgang: It's the same decision as whether to use a frame for a painting.

Ali: Yeah, it's like a frame.

Wolfgang: A form decision.

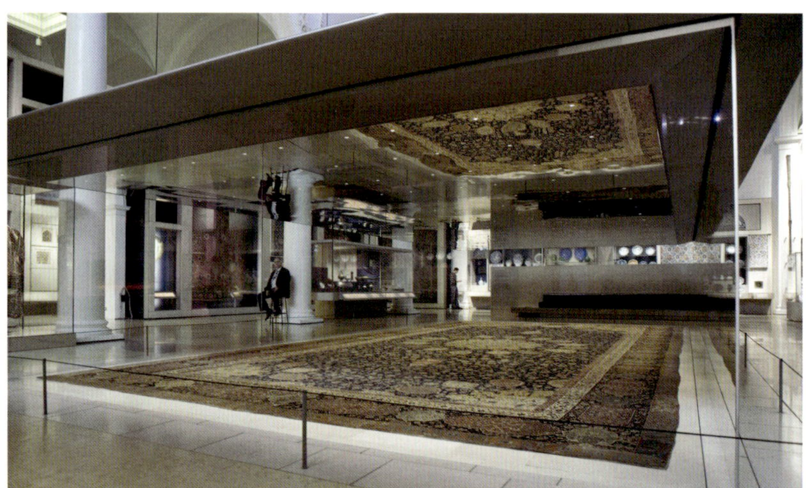

The Ardabil Carpet, Iran, 1539-1540, © Victoria and Albert Museum, London

Concerning the naked or nude costumes, what's the connection between nudity and shit?

Ali: Innocence.

Wolfgang: You don't know the profession of a person who is naked and looking at his or her shit. You don't know if this is a baker or gallerist.

Ali: Also, if you look at the shit of someone who is super rich…

Scott: Their shit doesn't stink?

Ali: No, their shit stinks as well.

Florian: It's also this Gelatin attitude that, when you place four very monumental, precise, sculptures in this neutral room, you look super classic and to adding an element that breaks this serious attitude is a move you make. It's a nice move to break the monumentality of the attitude. It breaks it and it makes it more accessible. It doesn't stand in front of you like a Richard Serra, "Bop! Big shit." You have to add something that creates a different mood.

Wolfgang: I like that everybody either really, really likes the naked suits, or hates them. It's so cheesy, but it's so nice as well, to please somebody, to be generous. Even people who don't like the shit like the clothes.

What aspect of the work does the museumgoer miss out on if he or she doesn't wear a naked costume?

Tobias: I think you can enjoy the exhibition whether you wear one or not.

Wolfgang: The show is called "Vorm – Fellows – Attitude" and the costumes are as well about attitude. You don't have to wear one, but get your shit together and get some attitude! Show some attitude. But it doesn't make it better or worse not to wear one.

Tobias: The sculptures don't care about the costumes.

Ali: You walk through the dressing room, you see the costumes, maybe you have heard people have worn the costumes, but you don't have to wear a costume yourself to understand and visualize it.

Tobias: It's not just you wearing the costumes. You see other people wearing the costumes and it's a nicer image to see other people in those costumes as you go around the show.

Florian: And you behave differently.

Tobias: Yeah, you behave differently.

Ali: If you wear one you have the chance to feel different; you feel different.

Wolfgang: When you wear these costumes, you kind of criticize your own exhibition. By bringing in these costumes it is a bit of a caricature…

Florian: …no, ridicule…

Wolfgang: …then you get away from this monstrous idea of the sculptural sizes. But it's a layer that really adds something, opens up something. Whether you wear them or not, you can choose how to wear them, and it's adding something. It's good to bring in an element that adds rather than limits.

Florian: I think, more and more, that this show has different elements, but it is more what you would call "a conversation piece." There are sculptures, there is this room, and then you walk through and it's a conversation piece. When you're not in an opening situation, you go in the show and there's maybe five or six people in the room. Not more. When you put on a naked costume and meet another person, who you don't know, in a naked costume, it's easier to start a conversation because you can give her or him a compliment on how good they look and how nice this is because you feel a bit insecure in your own naked costume. You start talking: "Here's *scheisse*, blah, blah, blah…" You're not cool. You're not in your suit, looking at sculptures. And people *do* start talking in this situation.

Wolfgang: The dialogue of the costumes and the people who wear them makes the people human again. Because, apparently, when you enter an institution, you play a role. This is something we could talk about, but we don't need to because we believe in the strength of the sculptures.

Ali: For me it's different. For me, you change your masquerade, you put another one on and are involved in a different kind of conversation.

Florian: Yeah, but when you are in a costume it's easier to start a conversation with a person you don't know.

Ali: I think that also what happens with the scale of the sculpture is that, because they relate so much with how we made them and your own size, your own body, and you recognize it's shit, you have this play of these oversized shits that are made to relate to your body to be gigantic and have this massiveness and you see other people running around in it and they have naked costumes, so you have a lot of play. It all works together.

Florian: You're in the outfit and you're immediately immersed in the situation.

Scott: So you're *in* the exhibition, in the work.

Florian: Yeah. You could put one hundred people in Chanel costumes and have all these people looking at this shit in these weird outfits and you could start a conversation. So the nudity is just one form, one form of dress.

Tobias: If you have a naked costume you become a participant instead of an audience. You are part of the show. It's very inclusive.

Ali: We also like this play with the naked costumes because you get dressed to be naked. You put another layer on to do what you usually do by taking layers off. So it's maybe a play with not being human. There's nothing that makes you human, it's all a costume. It's all play, the shit is real but the shit is not real.

Wolfgang: We don't have to explain what we are doing because we work out of our balls and stomach and heart, maybe more with balls and stomach, or asshole, whatever. We trust these organs more than the brain.

Florian: No, you don't have to explain it, but you can talk about where it comes from and the naked costumes come, actually, from a coincidence in Poland, where they happened, but also from a situation at Fondazione Prada where, when you go there, you realize that people really dress up to go and see a show. People there, visitors, are dressed super sharp. And then you develop an idea that, instead of dressing up for an opening, you "take away" the outfit. You dress them down again. But you dress them down in a very elegant way.

Ali: There are some artworks that are made so that you look good in front of them. It's this "backdrop" idea. With the shits…

Tobias: You look good out in front of the shits.

Ali: Everybody looks good in front of a shit but it's also not really a backdrop.

Scott: But this is a very "Instagramable"…

Ali: Only the small shit is Instagramable because you see everything in one image. All the other shits are too big.

Florian: It's a good backdrop, but for Instagram and photos it's too dark for a really good backdrop. A good backdrop is much lighter.

Ali: With a lot of color, hues and oranges…

Florian: Light ones, not brown, not black…

Wolfgang: I saw young kids in the show in Rotterdam and they were holding the naked-costume penis of their mother and they were definitely taking something home. The next time they shit they will want to go back to see the exhibition. Maybe this show is life changing for them…

Francesco Stocchi
Curator Modern and Contemporary Art
Museum Boijmans Van Beuningen

The mind has to catch up, in sex: indeed, in all the physical acts. Mentally, we lag behind in our sexual thought, in a dimness, a lurking, grovelling fear which belongs to our raw, somewhat bestial ancestors. In this one respect, sexual and physical, we have left the mind unresolved. Now we have to catch up, and make a balance between the consciousness of the body's sensations and experiences, and these sensations and experiences themselves. Balance up the consciousness of the act, and the act itself. Get the two in harmony. It means having a proper reverence for sex, and a proper awe of the body's strange experience. It means being able to use the so-called obscene words, because these are a natural part of the mind's consciousness of the body. Obscenity only comes in when the mind despises and fears the body, and the body hates and resists the mind.

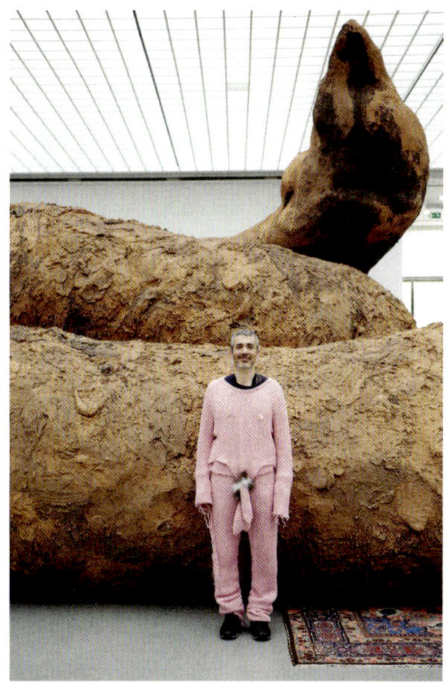

Thus affirms D.H. Lawrence in his essay "A Propos of 'Lady Chatterley's Lover'" a clarification and a defence of what is probably his best-known, and certainly most frequently discussed, novel; the one that best summarizes his philosophy.

Gelatin orchestrate the human passions—the love for what seems provocatively simple—like a modern-day D.H. Lawrence. While he extensively reflects, among other things, on the dehumanizing effects of modernity and industrialization, which led him to embrace and propound a "primitivist" attitude, Gelatin has—over a period of 25 years spent working together—developed a sophisticated and visceral attitude toward everything that surrounds it. Some of the issues most frequently explored by both Lawrence and Gelatin are those of sexuality, vitality, spontaneity, and instinct, and the examination of the incapacitating or debilitating taboos that accompany them.

Lawrence's radical opinions brought him many enemies and he suffered from the censorship and misrepresentation of his creative work. At the time of his death he was generally considered to be a pornographer that had wasted his considerable literary talents. It was in the industrial context of Nottinghamshire that Lawrence developed his hostility toward the mining industry that had dehumanized his father and destroyed the English countryside that he saw as his idyllic birthplace.

This hostility is also evident in *Lady Chatterley's Lover* and in the maledictions Lawrence launched against the forms of industrialism and modern technology that he felt had caused the breakdown and disintegration of genuine human experiences.

The actions, sculptures and environments of Gelatin similarly exist in a perpetual realm of creative becoming that is continually reinterpreted in the context of a critical reflection on moral conduct thrown into disarray by humor; always aiming to be the object of discussion. The situations that they present us with hint at an underlying nostalgia regarding a forgotten idyll, a state of childlike innocence reiterated in all its disruptive and unfiltered simplicity. There is a highly personalized approach to making and creating, with all the power and prerogatives that deskilling entails. In fact almost anyone could, in their own way, make such works, which are more of an enticement or provocation to do things in one's own way than a utopia. They are creations that respond to specific cultural situations invested with preconceptions, expectations and certitudes, and they elicit a flow of events that are activated by the participation of the public. The idea that lies at the root of each new project undergoes upheavals and changes dictated by improvisation, by free re-adaptation and stimuli from microenvironments that have been re-created. These works-in-progress are intimately bound up with the attitudes of the public and with the celebration of what one might call a "gallery of attitudes," since it gives ample room for various contrasting attitudes and opinions to be elaborated and expressed inasmuch as space allows.

The exhibition "Vorm – Fellows – Attitude" presents us with the spectacle of gigantic mounds of excrement inside the large Bodon Galleries of the Museum Boijmans Van Beuningen. Constructed *in situ* so that they could not exist in this form anywhere else, they dominate the exhibition spaces in which they are too big to be brought into or removed. Placed on fine Persian carpets, these colossal sculptures with their rich hues of brown seem to refer to a primordial dimension that prevails over any idealizing aspirations towards aesthetic beauty. Here improvisation, humor, and the attitude of theatrical freedom do not appear as nihilistic as they do in a movement such as Dada, which was far more sensitive to aesthetic aspects. Gelatin blends all this with an ostentatiously frivolous, vital paradigm.

The creation of the four sculptures that occupy the 1,200 square meters of the museum's galleries required a collective task of fabrication and assembly that effectively overturned the canonical role of the museum as an institution intended solely as a venue for display and exhibition, temporarily transforming it instead into a place of artistic production, collective endurance, and *ménage*. This contemporary version of the ancient artist's workshop, entailing an approach based on autarchic inspiration, thus took concrete possession of these spaces so that the sculptures could be made directly inside the rooms where they were to be exhibited. In a subversion of the precepts of modernism, the artistic object is seen as having no importance as such, but is intended to facilitate physical congregation, encourage correspondences, and emphasize variations. It thus operates as a device for creating a relational environment and transforms the museum into a contemporary *agora*. After all, as the Greek philosophers pointed out, although the *polis* of Athens was a physical place with houses, markets, temples, and theaters, it was the living people of Athens who truly constituted the *polis*. The work of Gelatin therefore cannot be separated from its social function and truly comes to life thanks to the will of the visitor and beholder to become an active participant, challenge moral impositions, and let spontaneity prevail over well-established institutional codifications. In this appropriation of the museum's environment, norms and conventions, and in this breaking down of the boundaries between the traditional "Hall of the Muses" and the everyday world, there is no room for detached contemplation and the traditional quasi-religious approach to artwork. Beyond the despotic and absolutist artwork-visitor axis, the human body becomes the substance that allows the artistic artifact to be completed.

This entails a reciprocal exchange, since an all-encompassing immersion in the artistic dimension encourages self-reflection and a reconsideration of oneself and one's reaction toward external stimuli, like a sort of social therapy. The expressive modality of Gelatin does not lead to the production of a finished object so much as to an attitude; to the desire to communicate a way of doing and a vision of reality in which the individual prevails thanks to the celebration of their own idiosyncrasies. An apparent absence of rules turns the free will of the person and his or her uniqueness into a protagonist in such a way that the characteristics that distinguish each individual are welcomed as values and benefits that can expand and diversify our relationship with the artwork. In "Vorm – Fellows – Attitude" the public interacts with enormous heaps of matter by wearing a costume that simulates a naked body. The concept of wearing nudity is a desecrating and provocative idea that forces us to deal directly with an aspect of ourselves that is natural and familiar and yet constantly denied and repudiated.

This activity of dressing up involves a decision to get involved and participate, to step onto the stage without a definitive screenplay and together become ridiculous clownish actors, symbolic fools, or anti-heroes. The dynamics that are established between the sculptures and the visitor are comparable to those between theatrical scenery and actors. Like masks in Greek theatre, the nude costumes that museum visitors choose to wear allow them to slip into another identity, transforming them into something else and, at the same time, symbolically making them naked. These costumes of all possible genders, in various different skin colors and sizes, represent a filter for looking at reality with an approach that does not conform to our automatisms and in which the body is the protagonist and a means for exploration and knowledge. Nudity, both ostentatious and fictitious, unites the participants in a sort of collective participation, where their perplexity and naturally modest embarrassment are replaced by acceptance and active involvement, permitting the complete fruition of works that create new spaces within the museum.

This represents a symbolic return to the origins of life itself; to early childhood and the absence of the conditionings typical of adulthood, in a playful and ironic relationship with a substance that is an inevitable and ubiquitous product of life, but kept hidden and almost invisible within society at large. The intention is not to honor something that is our waste product *par excellence* by means of its monumental representation, but to create the right conditions through which it can be seen as a tribute to inclusion. This can be realized only when people become active participants rather than mere passive spectators. The subversion or overturning of hierarchies allows for the celebration of a waste substance in which we can all take part, thereby deflecting any possibility of creating an elitist form of art. The expressive modalities used by Gelatin are placed in relation to an audience that is as broad and diverse as possible, overturning conventions and the established order without proposing definitive solutions. Questions are posed about shared conceptions and morals without ever offering ethical judgments, while the rules are reshuffled and mixed up by an experiment that creates an autonomous micro-society, not based on a nihilistic or iconoclastic attitude of rejection of the rules, but on self-regulation. The language adopted by Gelatin intends to demystify art and use immediacy and clarity of intent as a communicative force, laying the foundations on which to engage in an ontological reflection so that we can take responsibility for our own actions, or as Candide puts it: *"Il faut cultiver notre jardin."*

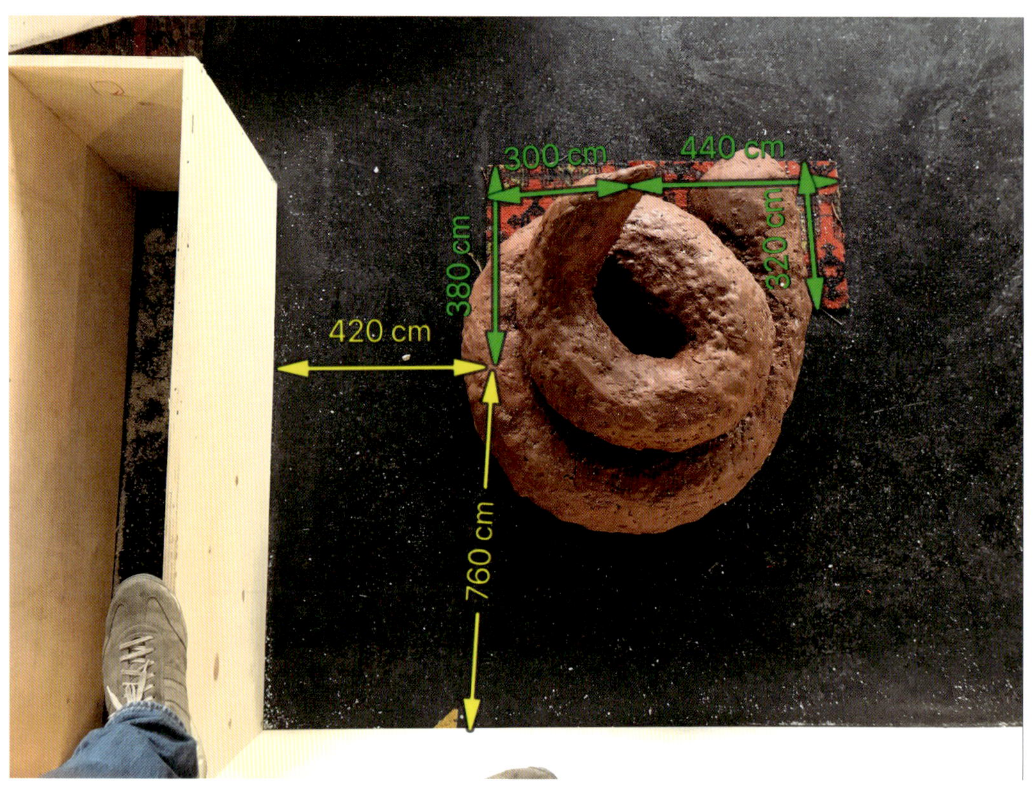
300 cm
440 cm
380 cm
320 cm
420 cm
760 cm

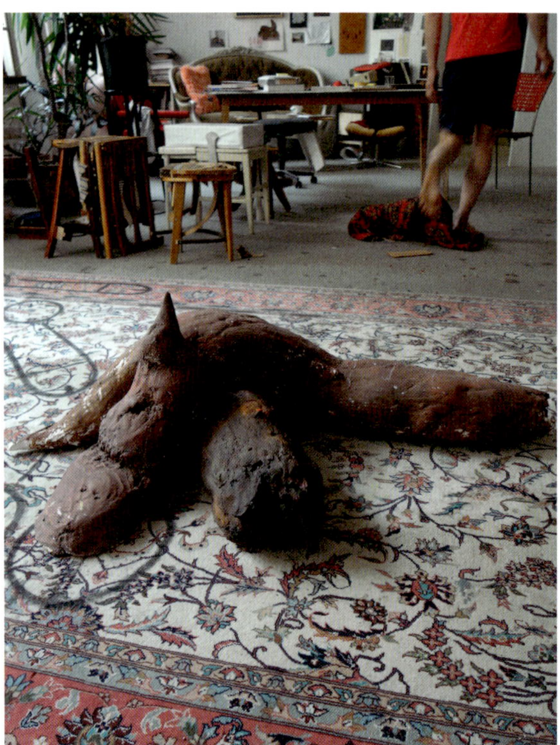

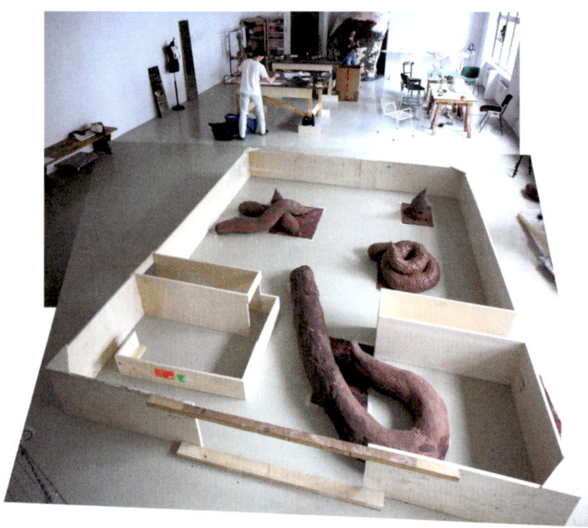

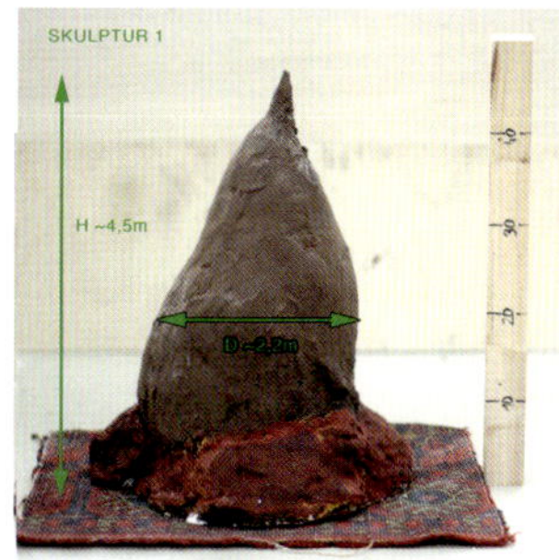

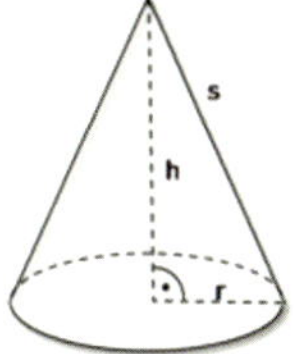

V Kegel = $1/3 * \pi * r^2 * h$

O Kegel = $\pi * r^2 + \pi * r * s$

O Kegel = $\pi * r^2 + \pi * r * \mathrm{WURZEL}(r^2 + h^2)$

	h	r (in Meter)
	3,9	1,3

V=   6,90 m3
O =   22,10 m2

braun-53	Hell 1	0,20	133 Liter
rot-38	Mittel 2	0,80	530 Liter
rot-38/G3 Sondermischung	Dunkel 3	0,00	0 Liter

Lehm Putz Oberfläche
Putzstärke

3 cm	663 Liter	1 Big Bags (1t)
2 cm	442 Liter	1 Big Bags (1t)

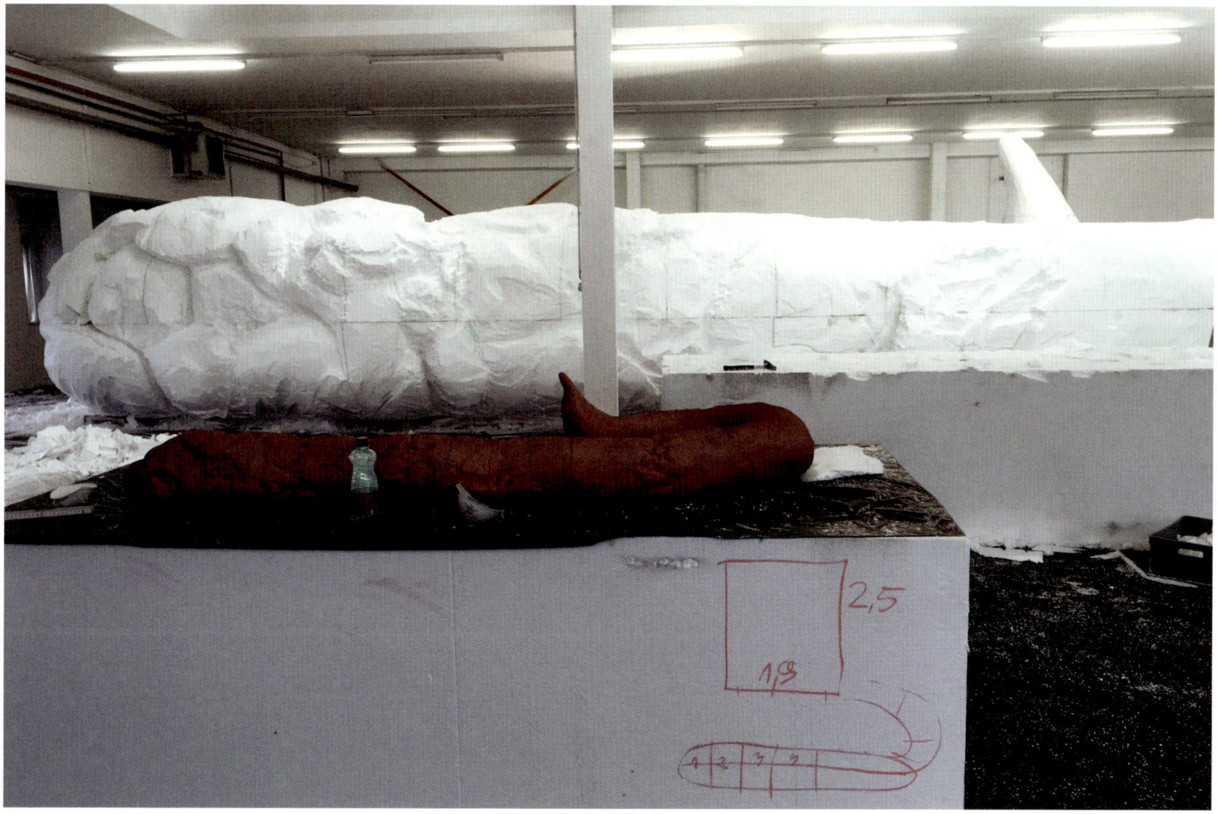

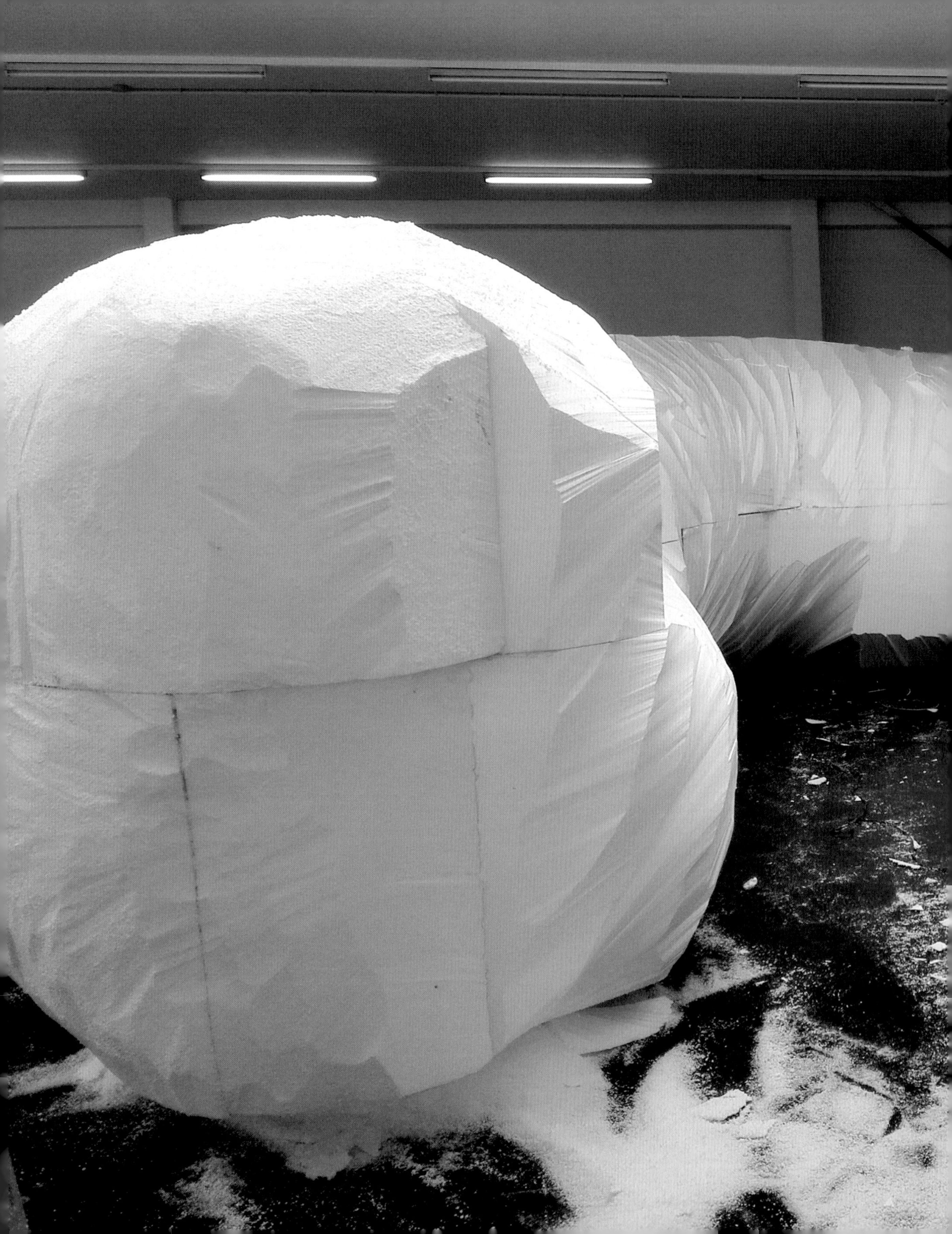

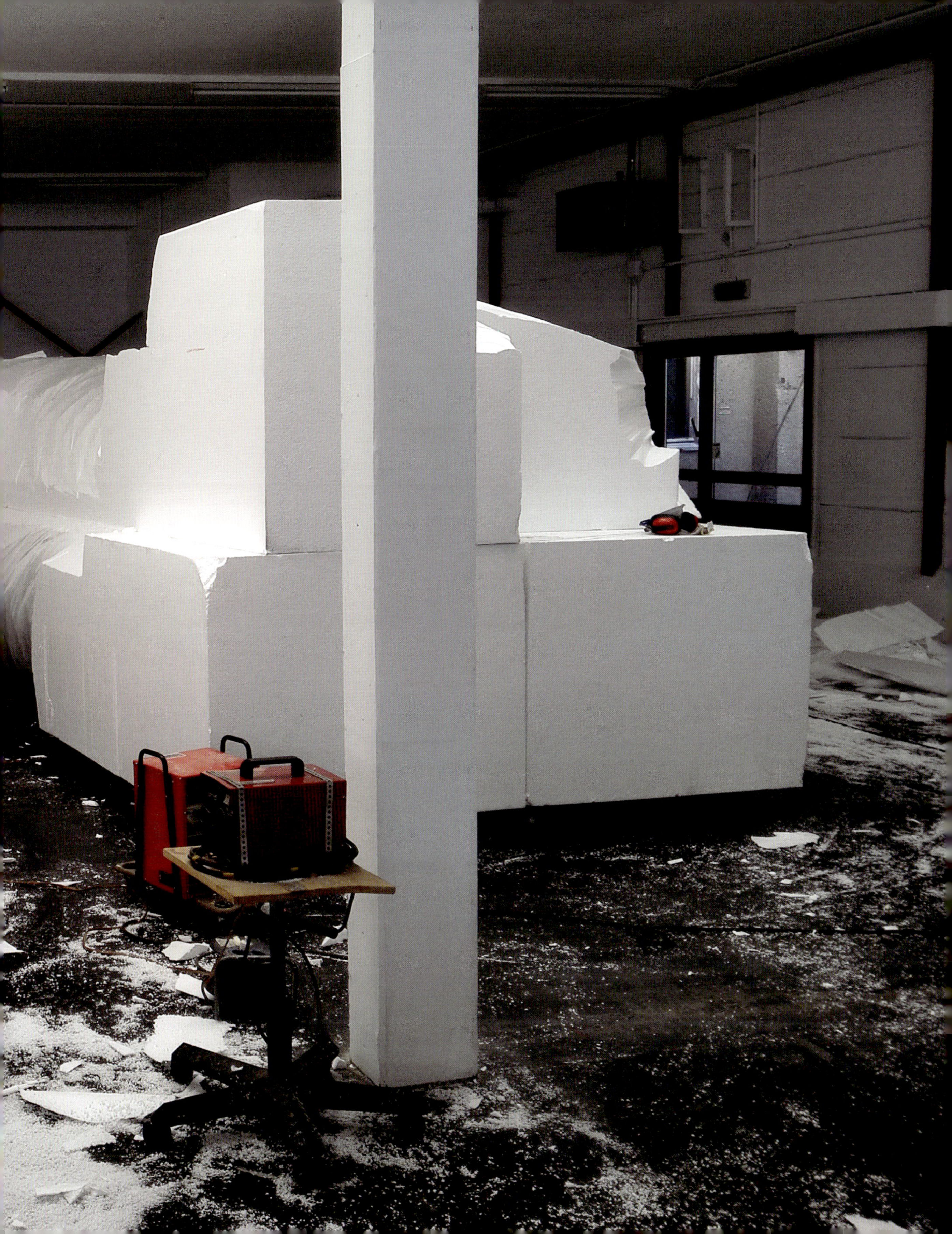

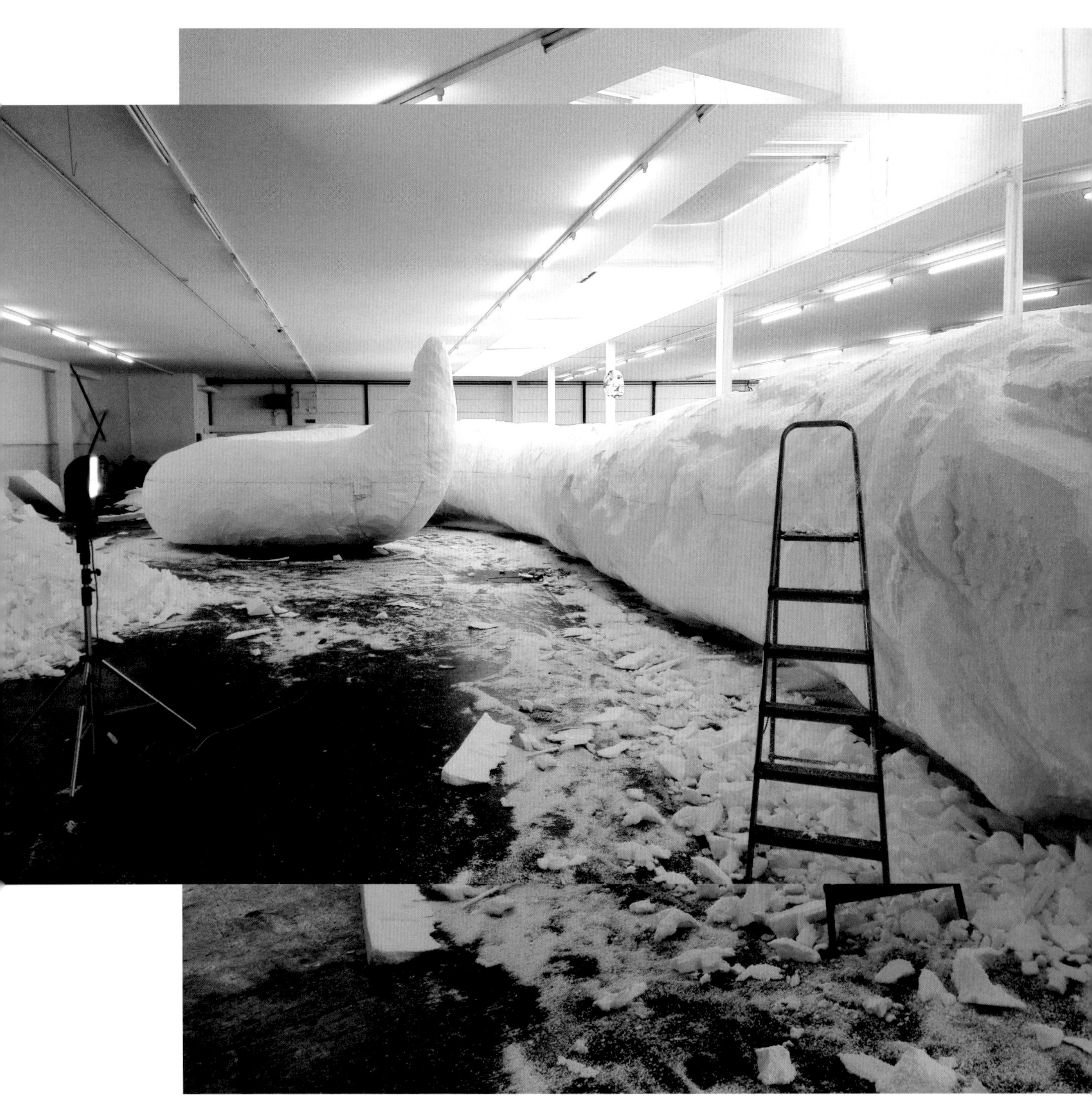

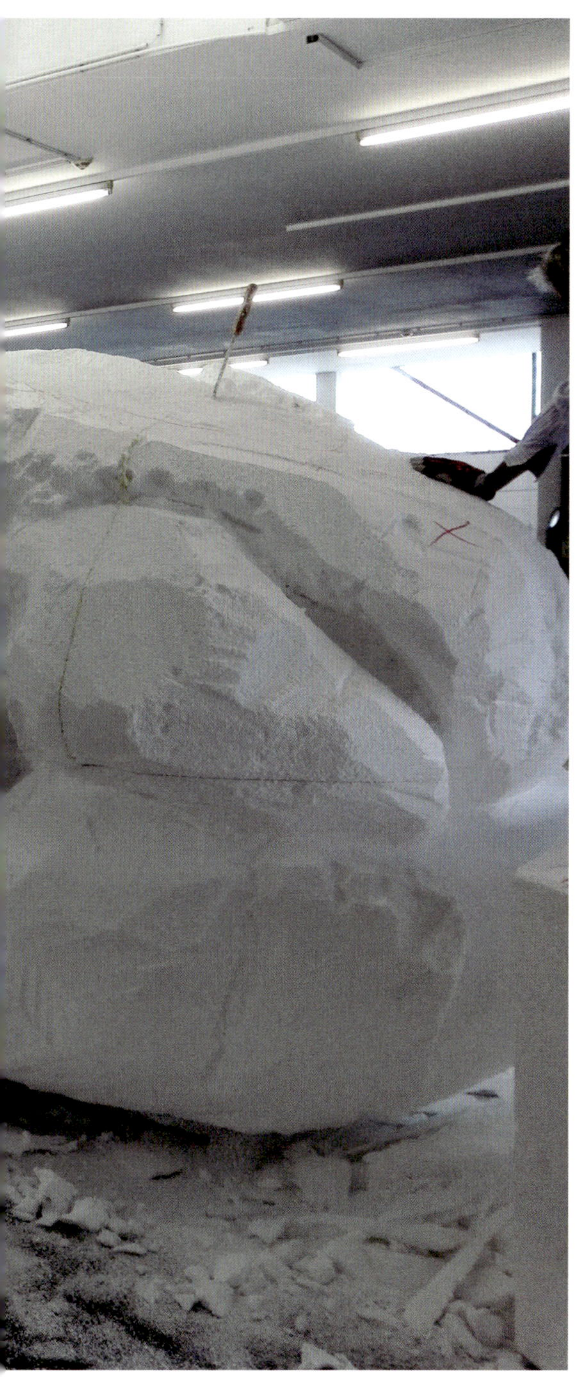

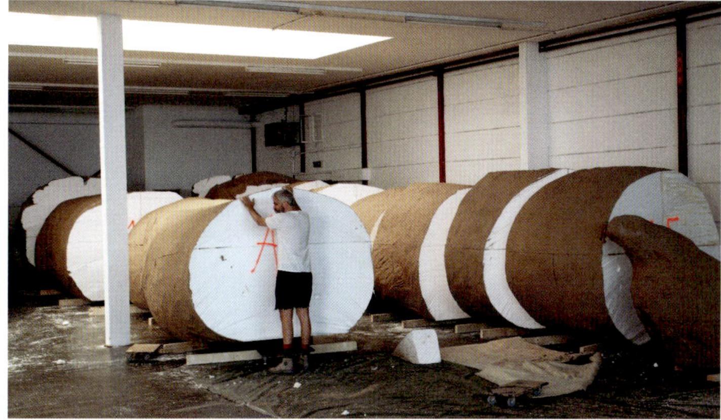

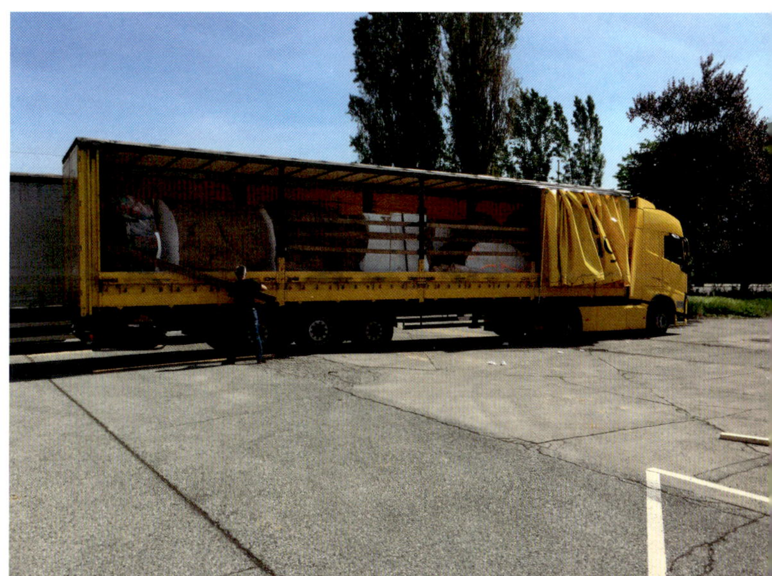

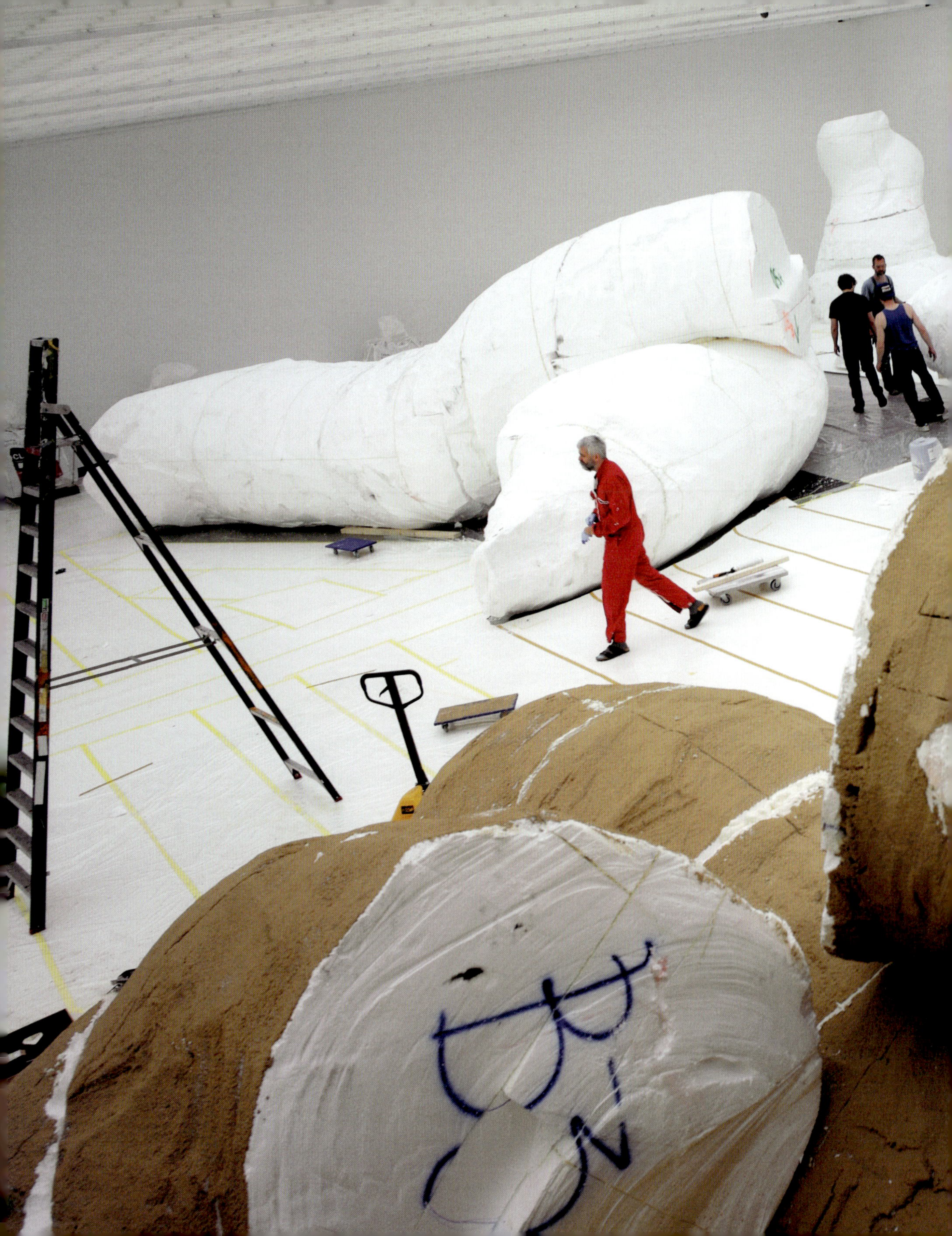

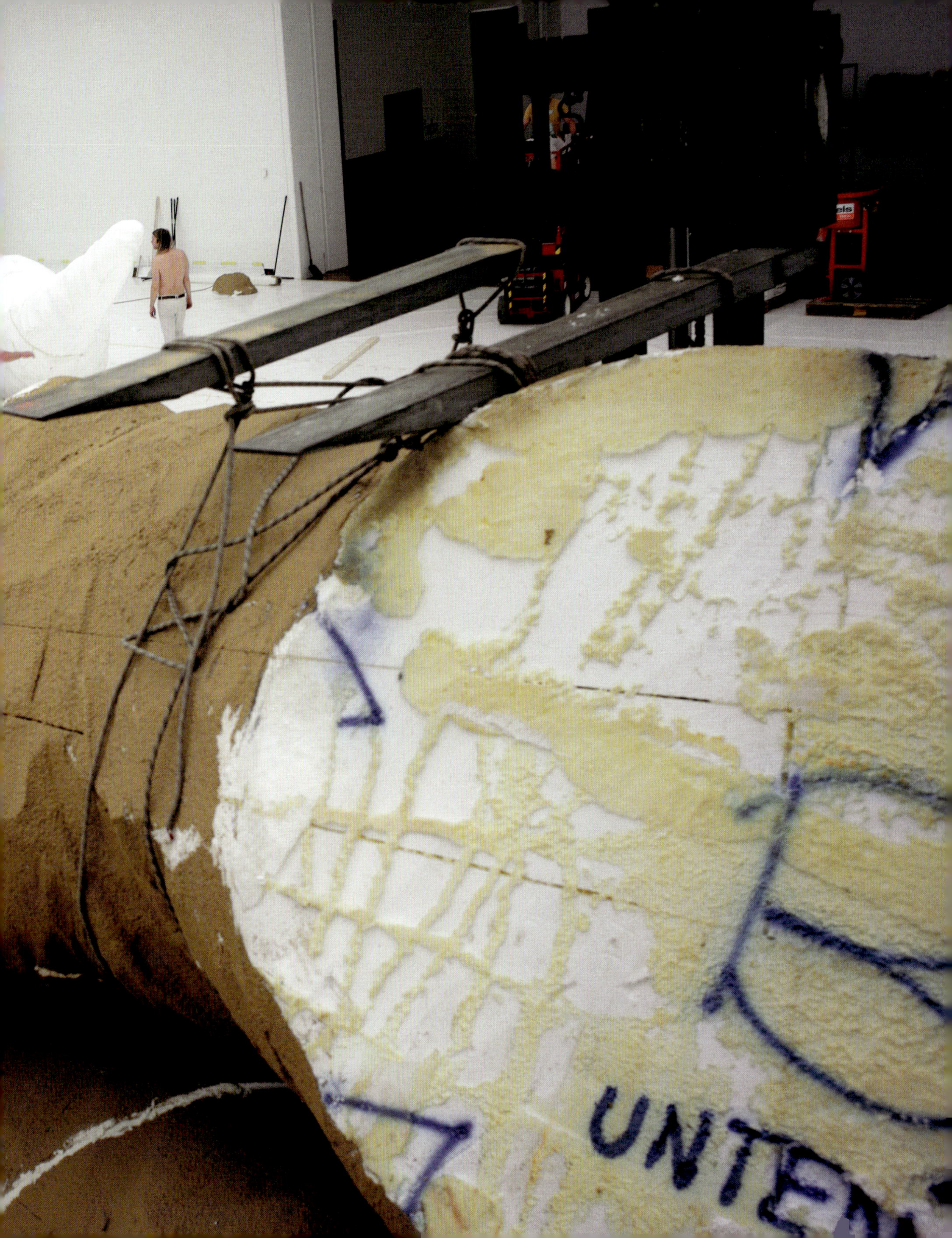

UNTEN

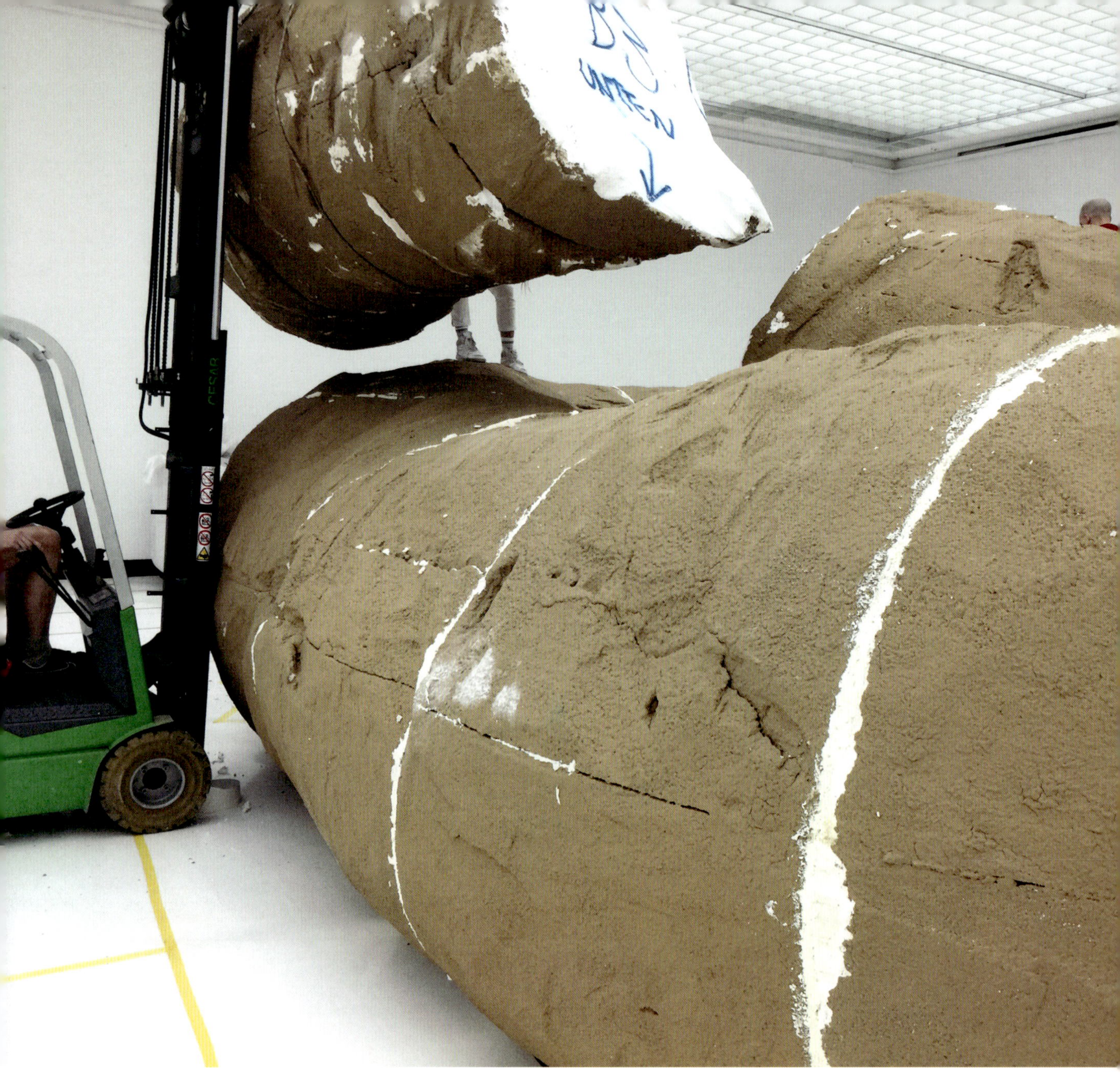

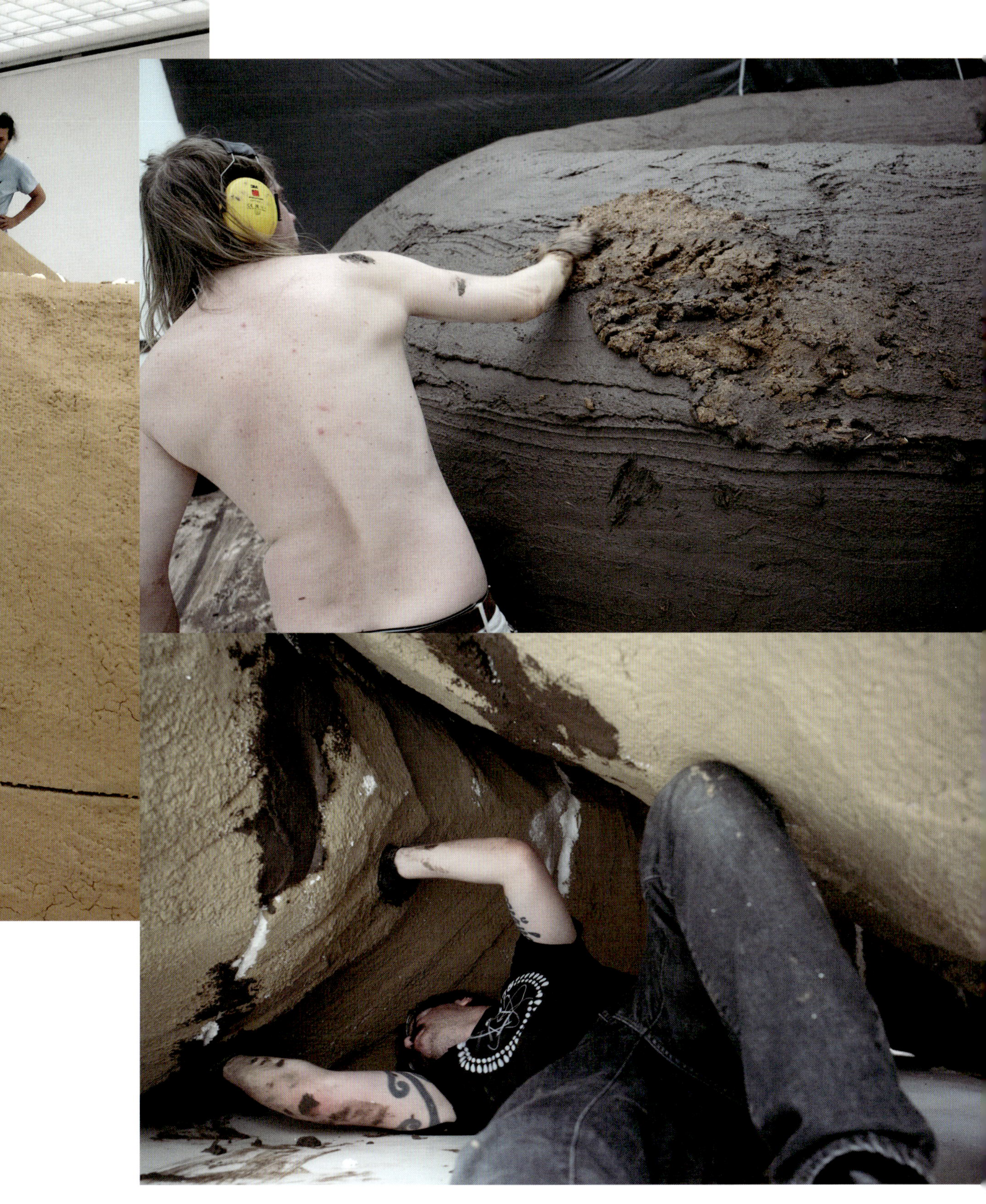

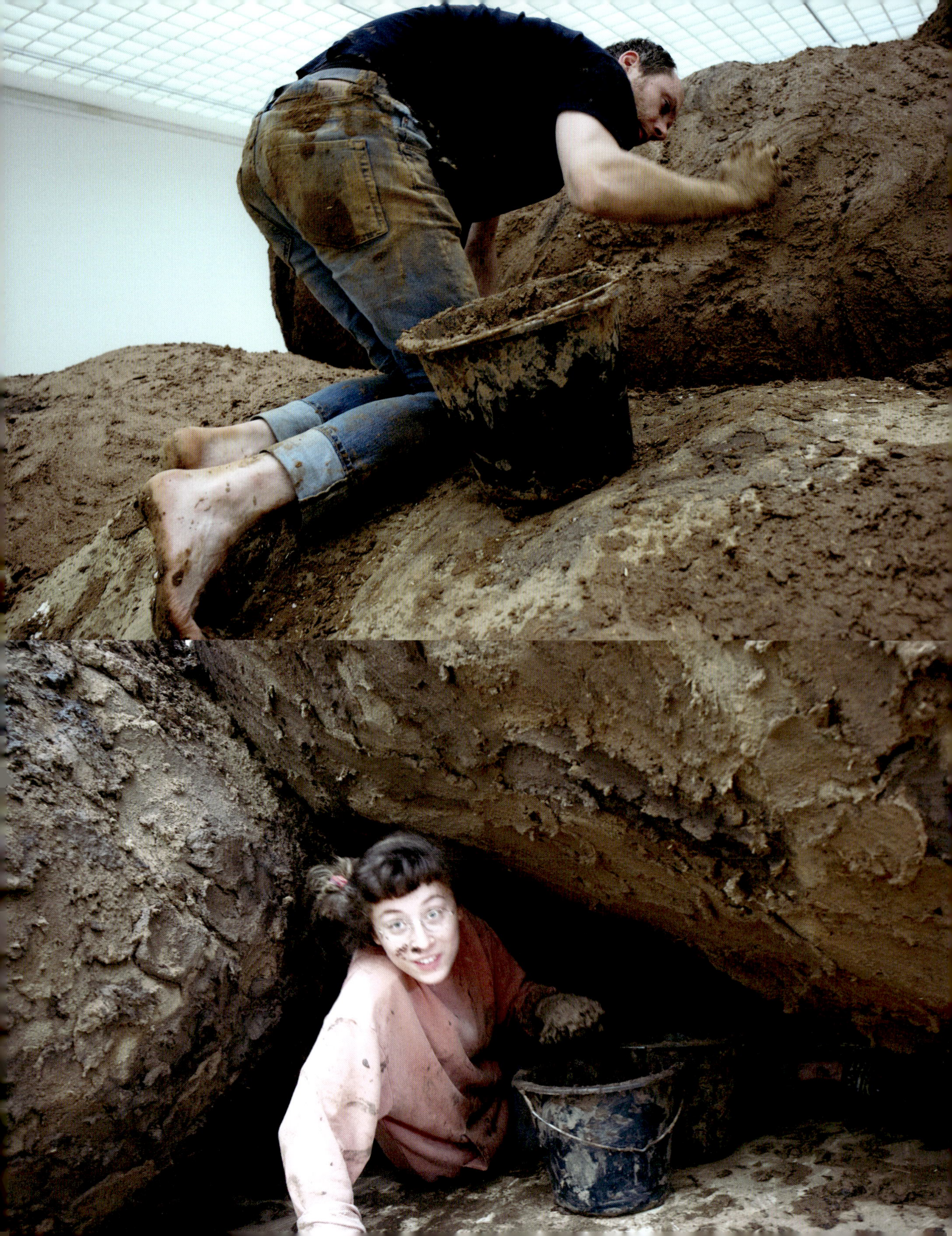

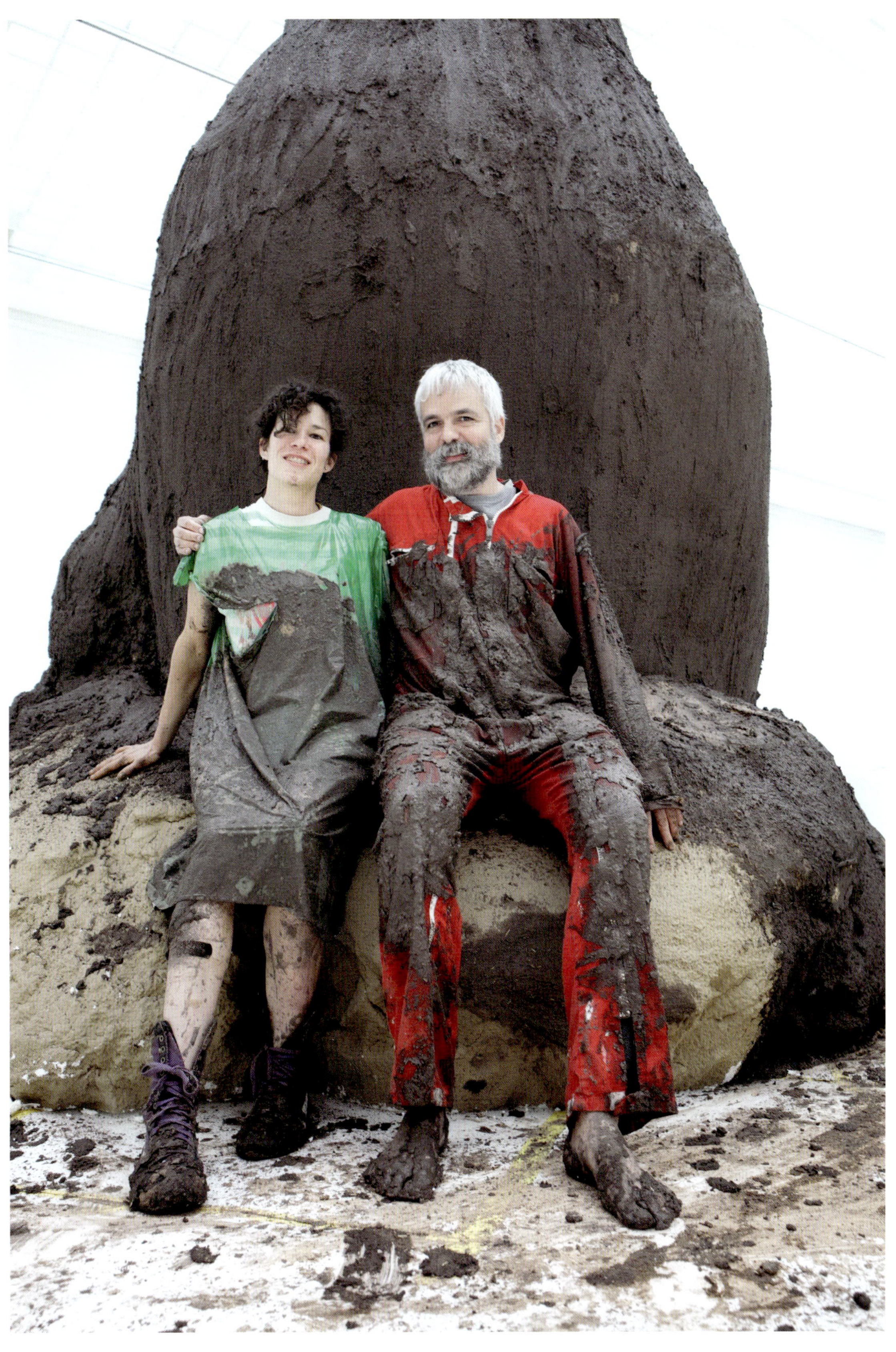

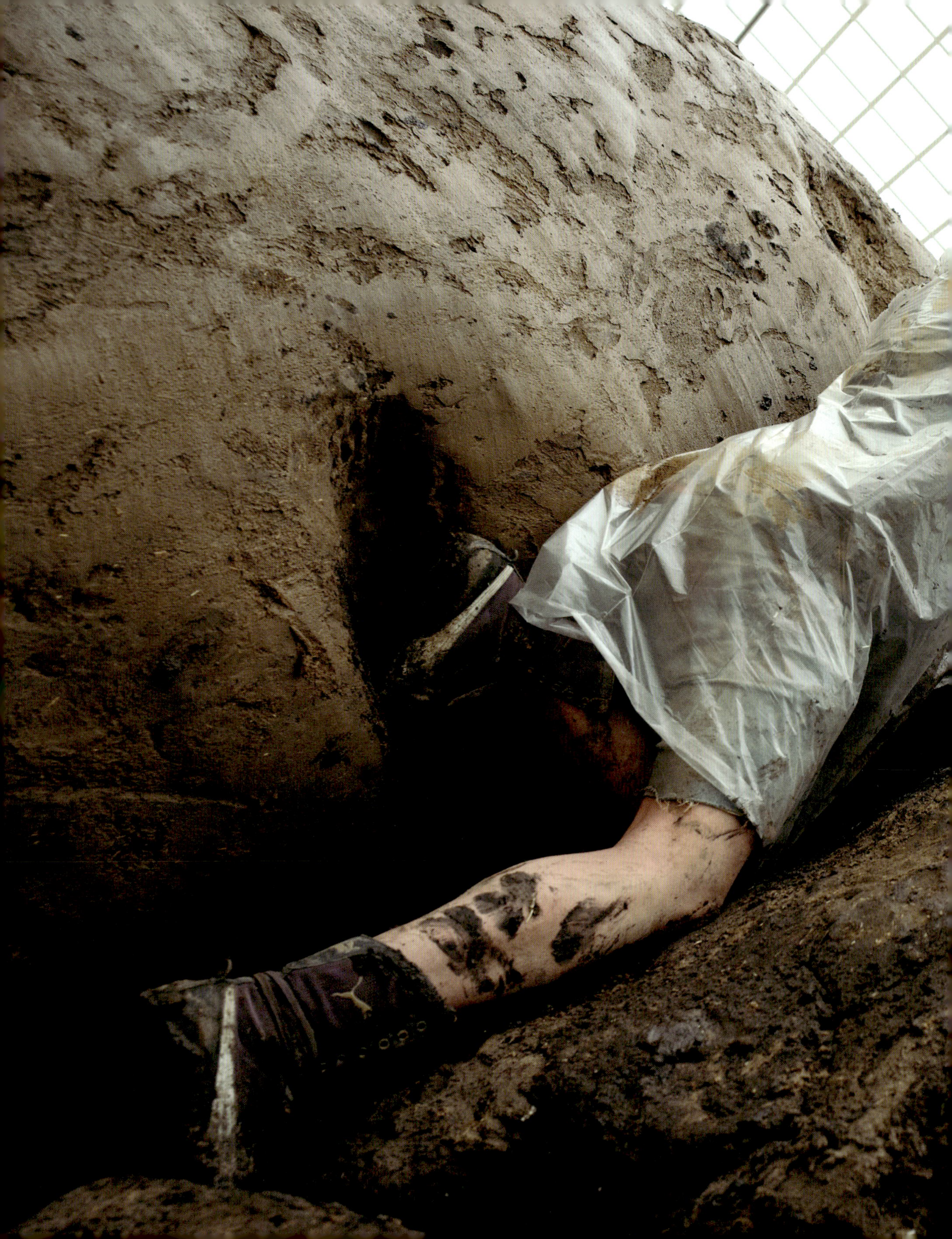

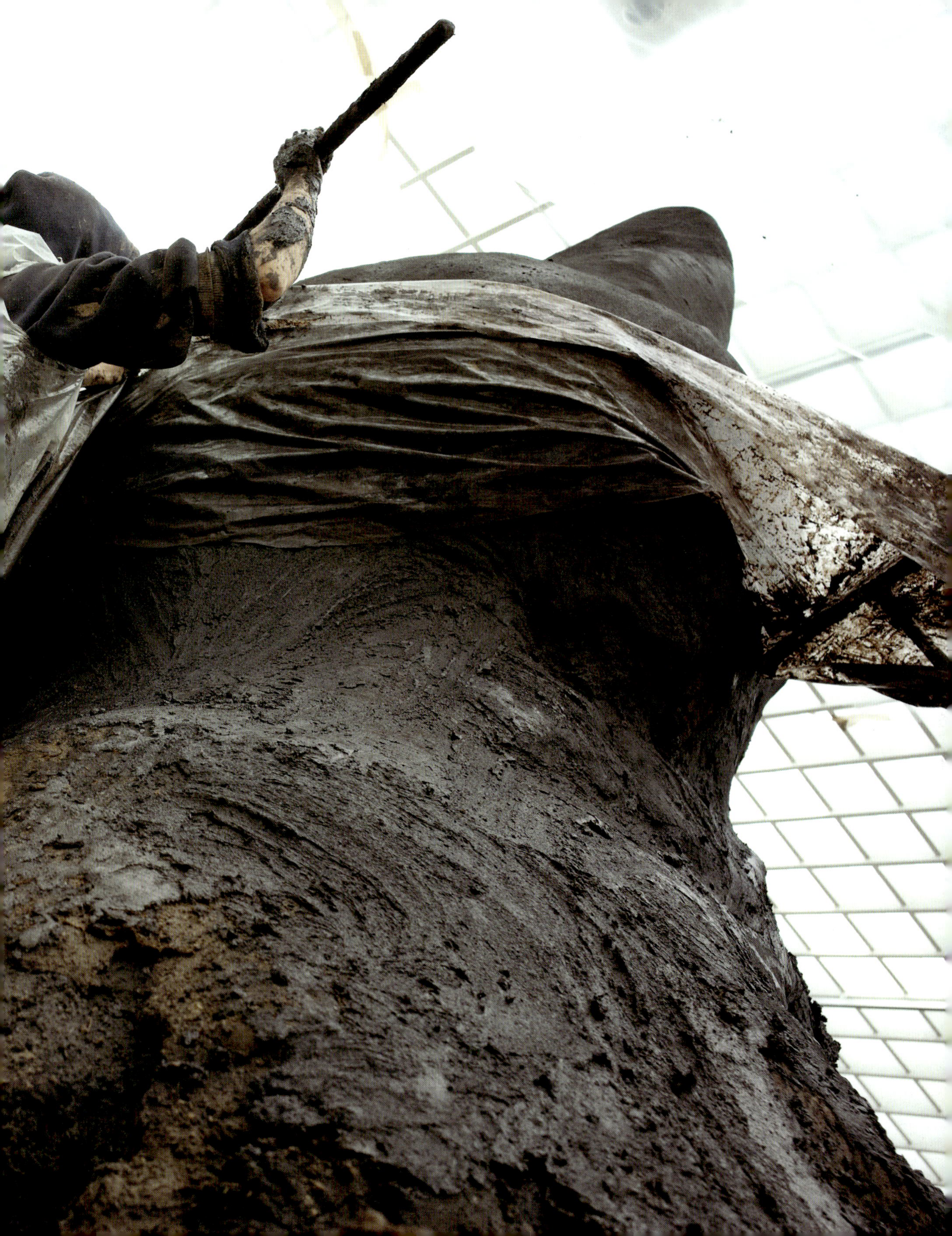

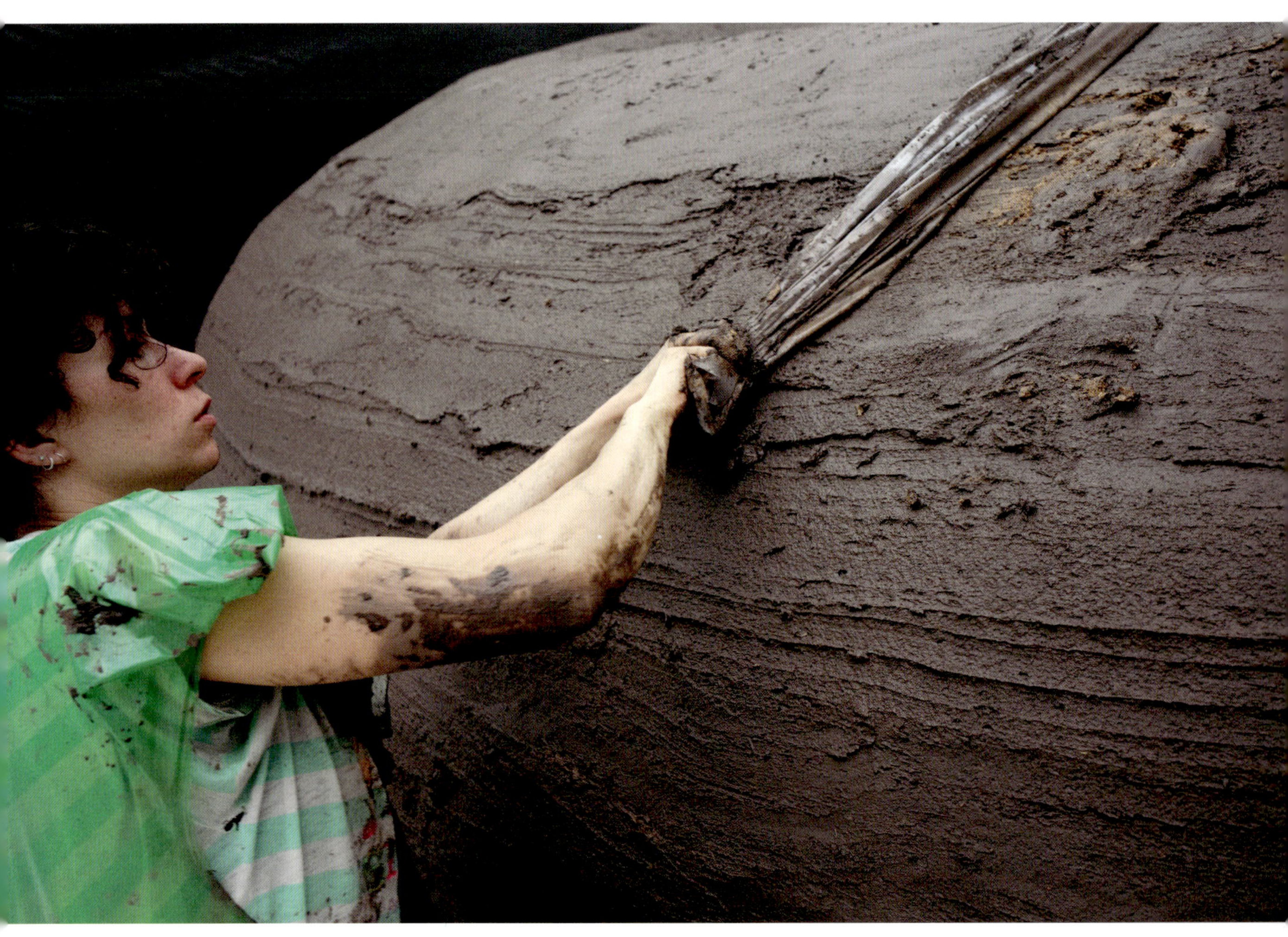

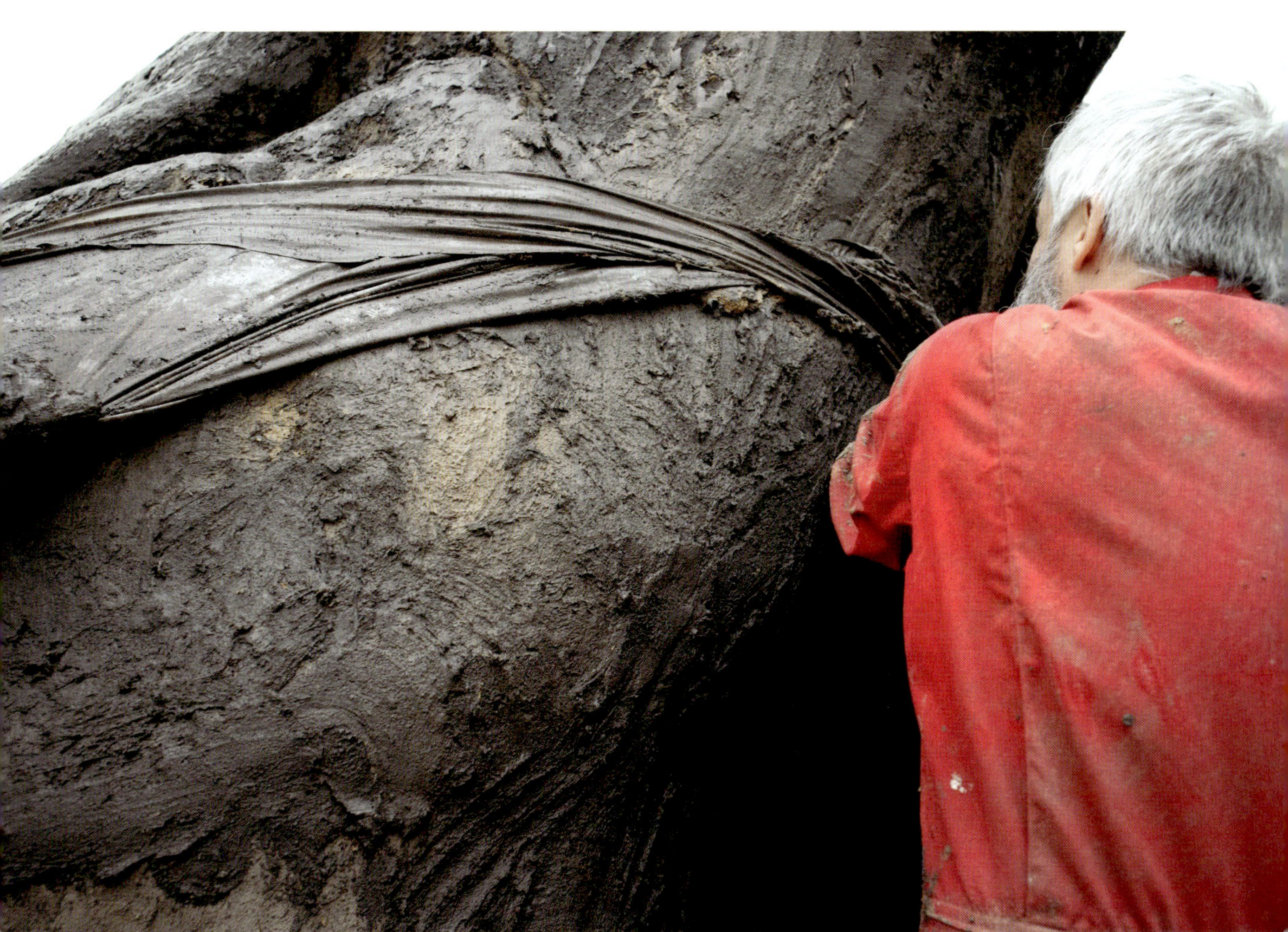

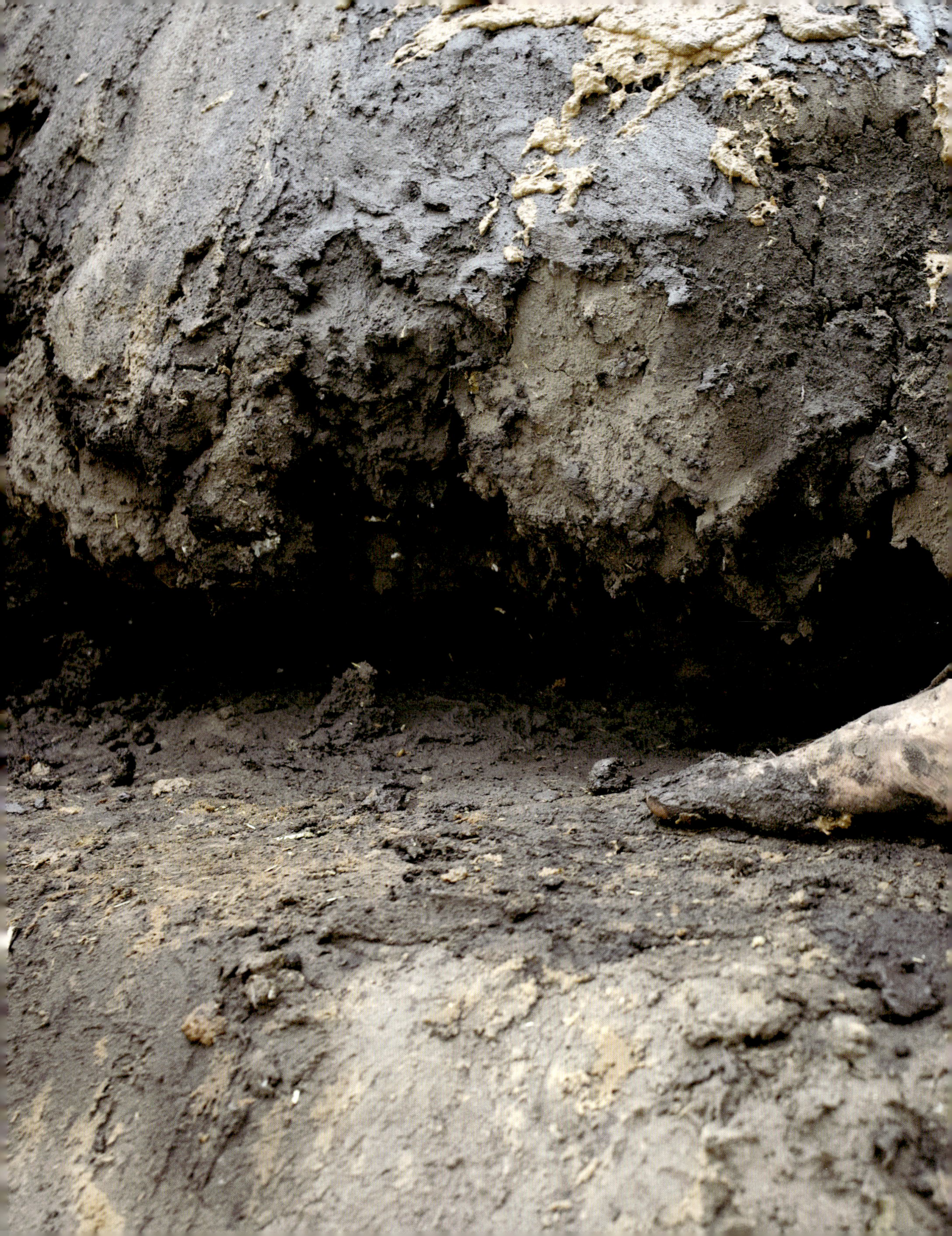

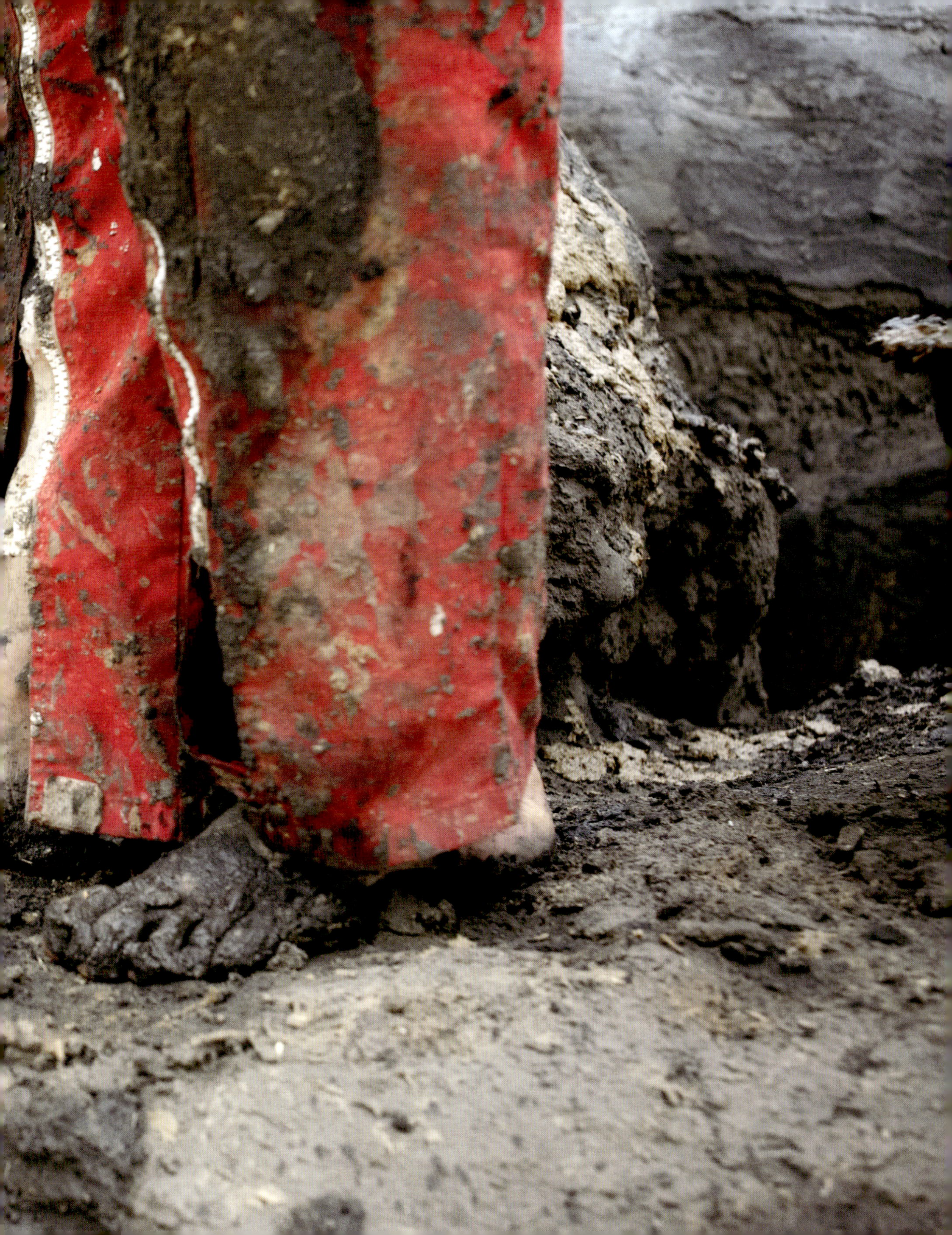

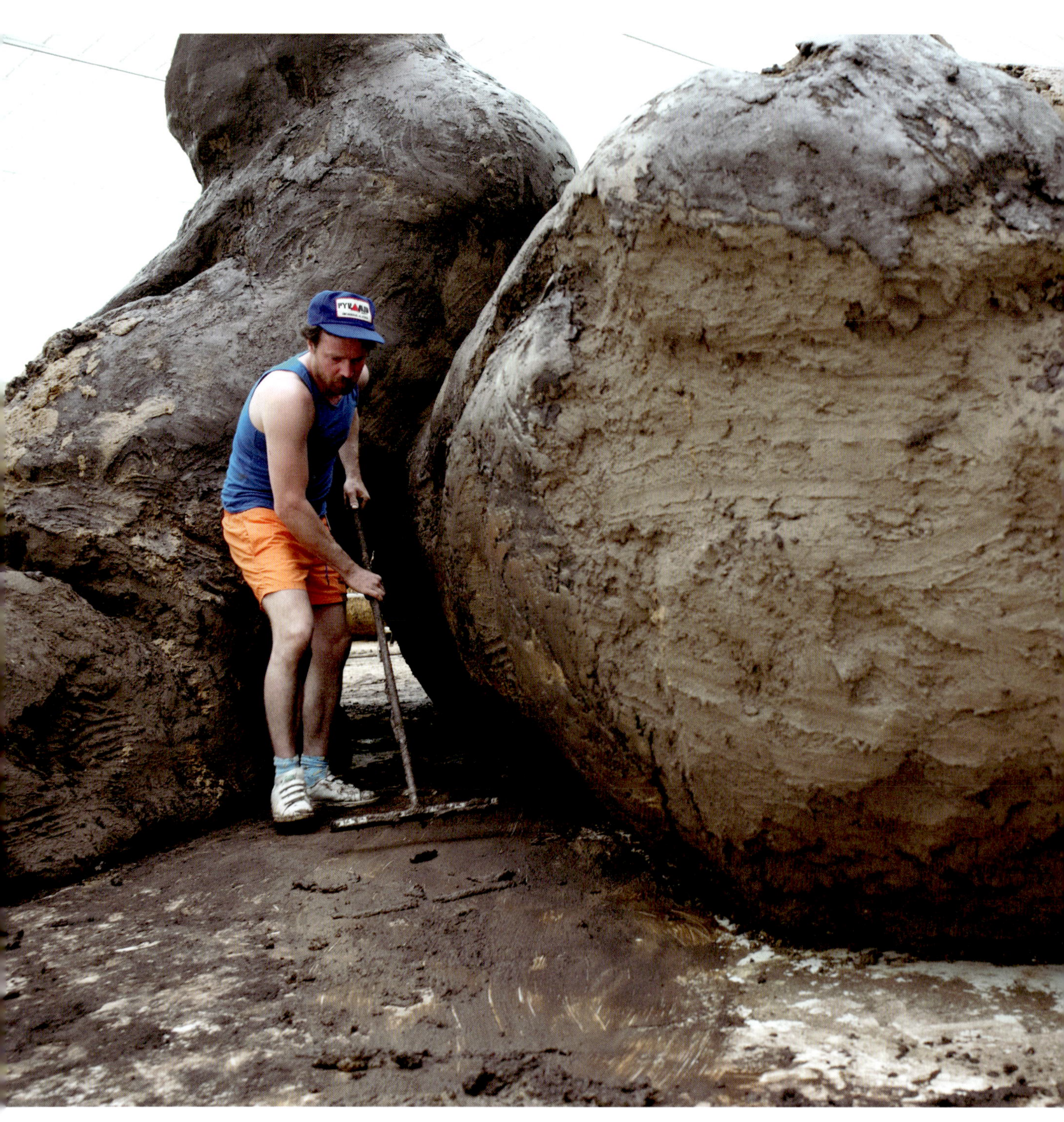

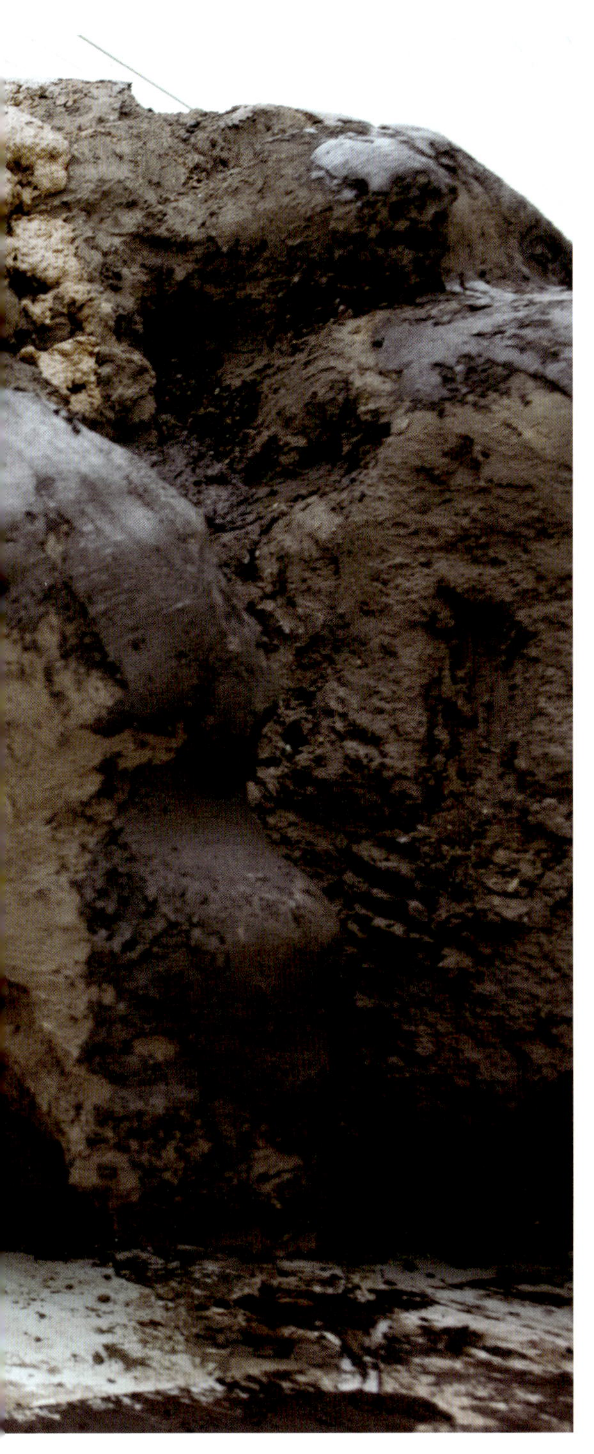
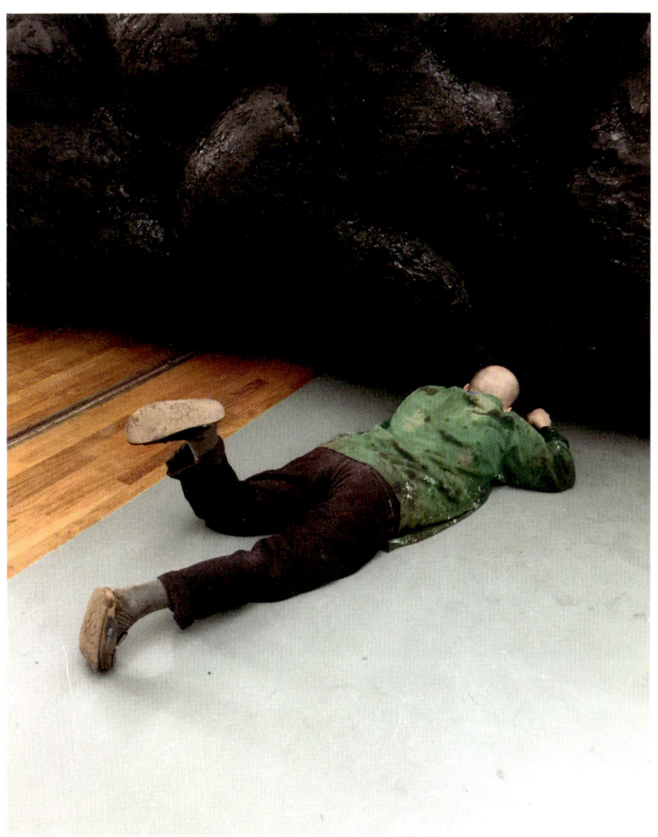

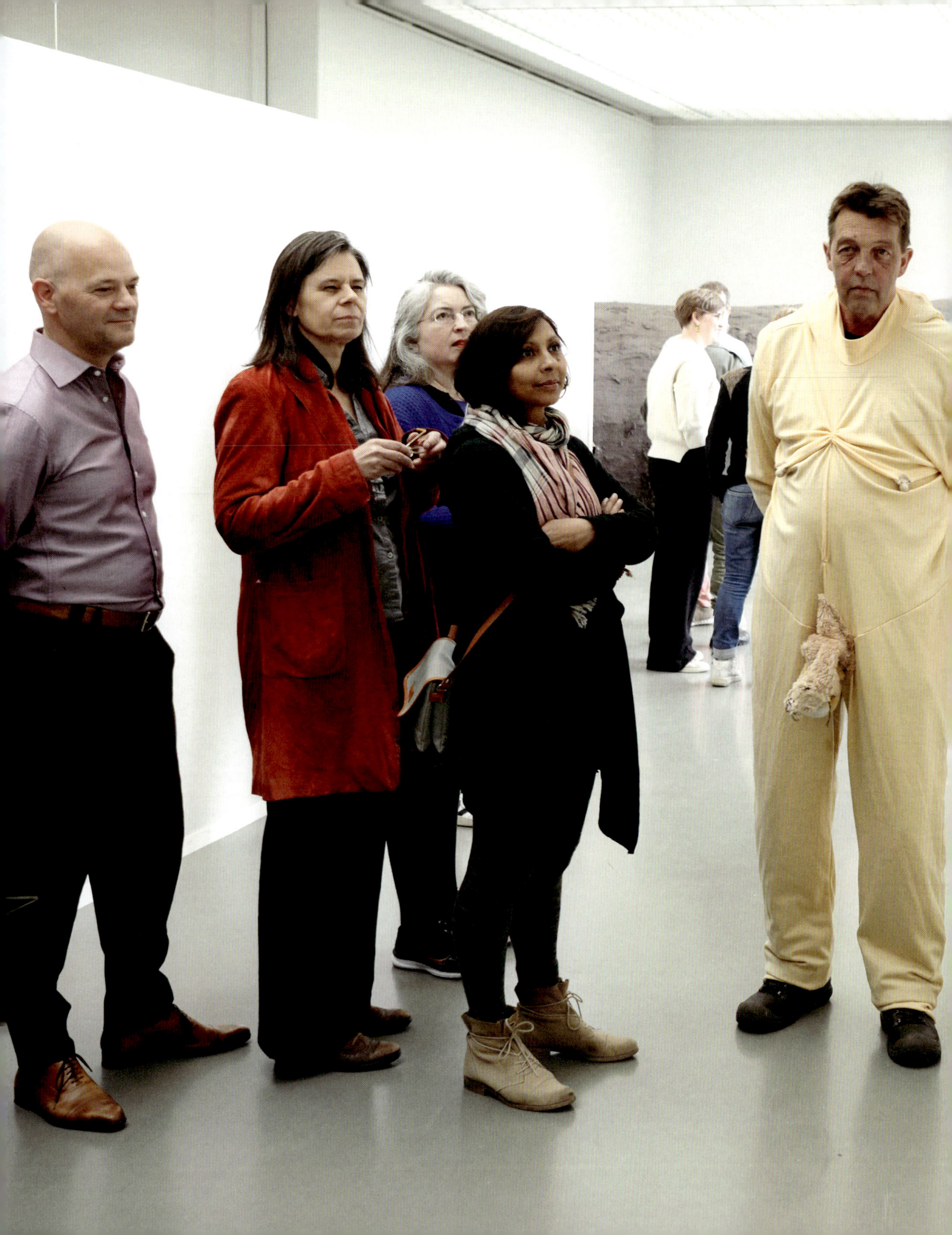

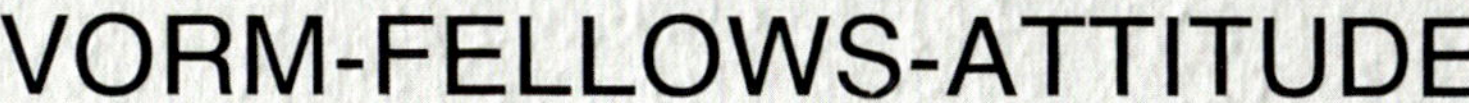

VORM-FELLOWS-ATTITUDE

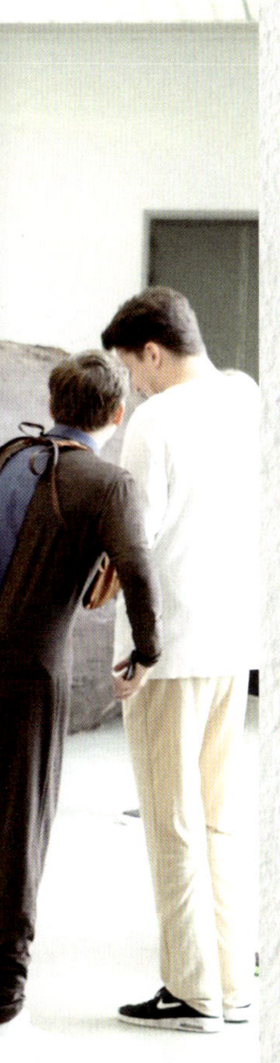

'Oui, by the love of my skin
I shit on Your nose
So it runs down Your chin'

Wolfgang Amadeus Mozart

RUGS, COLOSSAL TURDS, DOODOO BEASTLY EXCREMENT.
FEAST OF MERDA D´ARTISTA AND NUDITY.
ANALCONDA WASTE OF TIME IN A TURD WORLD.

'Stercus cuique suum bene olet'
'Everyone's shit smells good to himself.'

 Erasmus of Rotterdam

DIRT LOAF EXTRUSION VOIDING IN A BOWEL MOVEMENT.
DEMOCRATIC SCULPTURE FERTILIZER GELATIN.
CRAP ON A RUG, MASSELTOV AND BE NICE TO YOUR MAMA.

'Shit has to be encountered in another way. It's now necessary to rethink the
usefulness of the unuseful, the productivity of the unproductive, philosophically
speaking to unlock the positivity of the negative and to recognize our responsibility
also for what is unintended.'

Peter Sloterdijk

THIS IS ALSO A SHOW FOR ALL WHO THINK THAT CONTEMPORARY ART IS SHIT.
THEY SHOULD COME AND SEE THIS SHIT SHOW.
THEY WILL BE SATISFIED.

BRING YOUR FRIENDS AND FAMILY, RIDE THE BROWN SLUG TO WALHALLA.

Gelatin is four artists who started working together in 1993. In this exhibition, Gelatin
explores the disparate possibilities of what sculpture can be, disarming taboos that
cause prejudice, discomfort, and fear.

Met / With: Christoph Harringer, Anna Schwarz, Bert Löschner, Manuela Scheiwiller,
Helmut Heiss, Olga Wukounig, Scott Clifford Evans, Martina Noskova, Kolbeinn Hugi
Höskuldsson, Olivia Reither, Tom Van Camp, Iris Schuttevaar, Jason Schmidt, Manó
Dániel Szöllösi, Lili Ullrich, Mario Gamser, Jackie Lee, Mahyar, Josefine Reither,
Roland Klima, Sue van Geijn, Gerhard Riml, Familie Levinitschnig, Georg Holzmann,
Jan Weiler, Hermann Fink

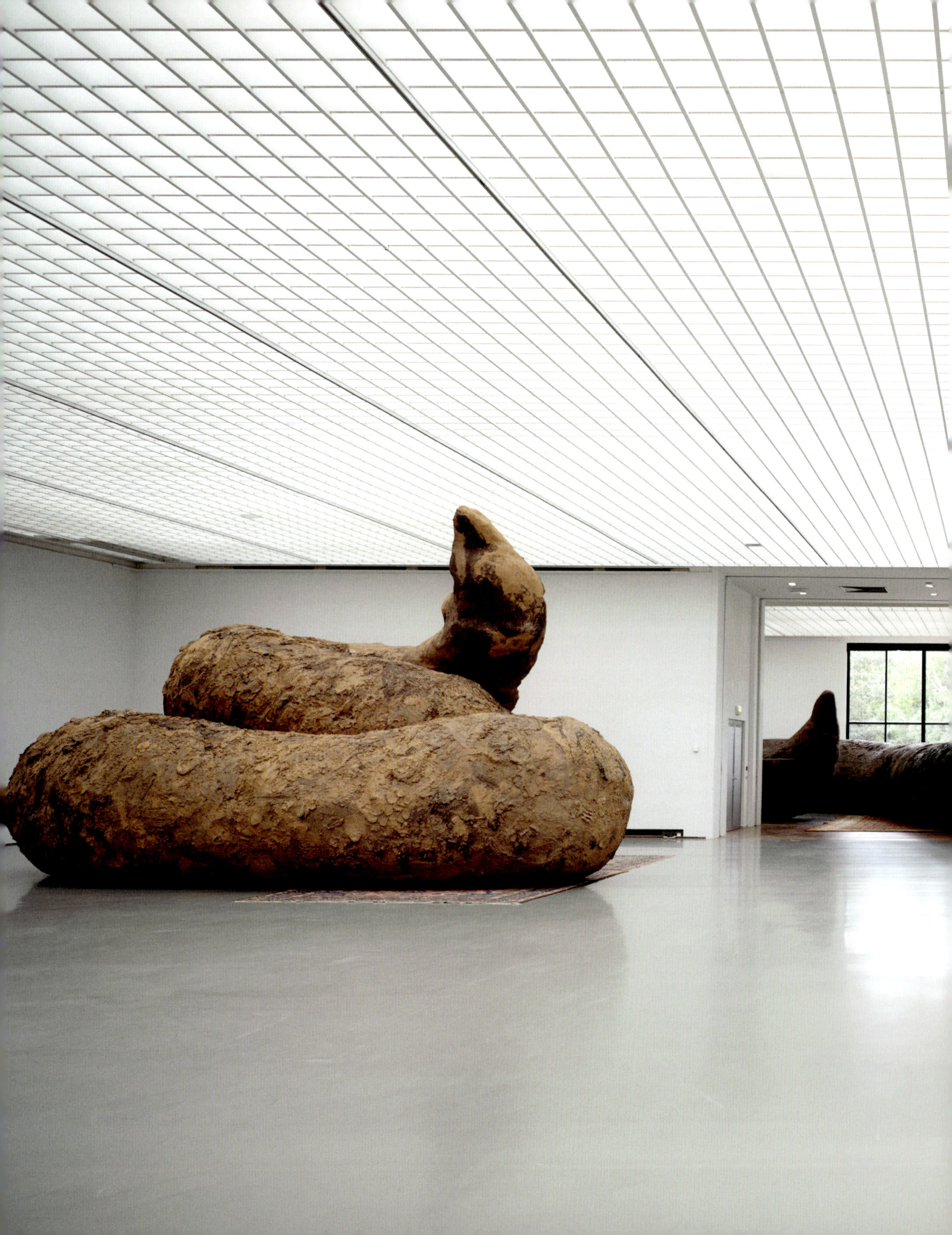

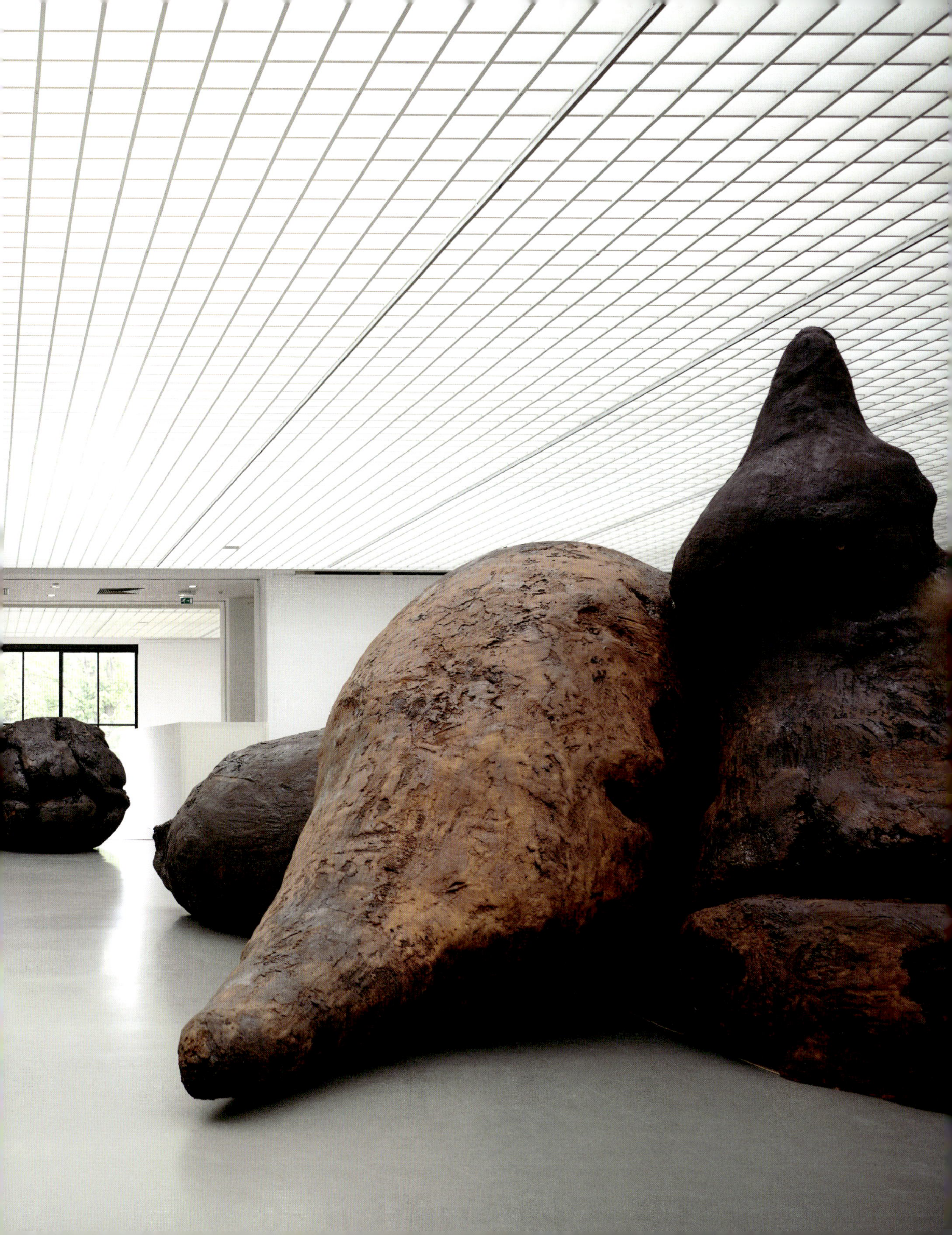

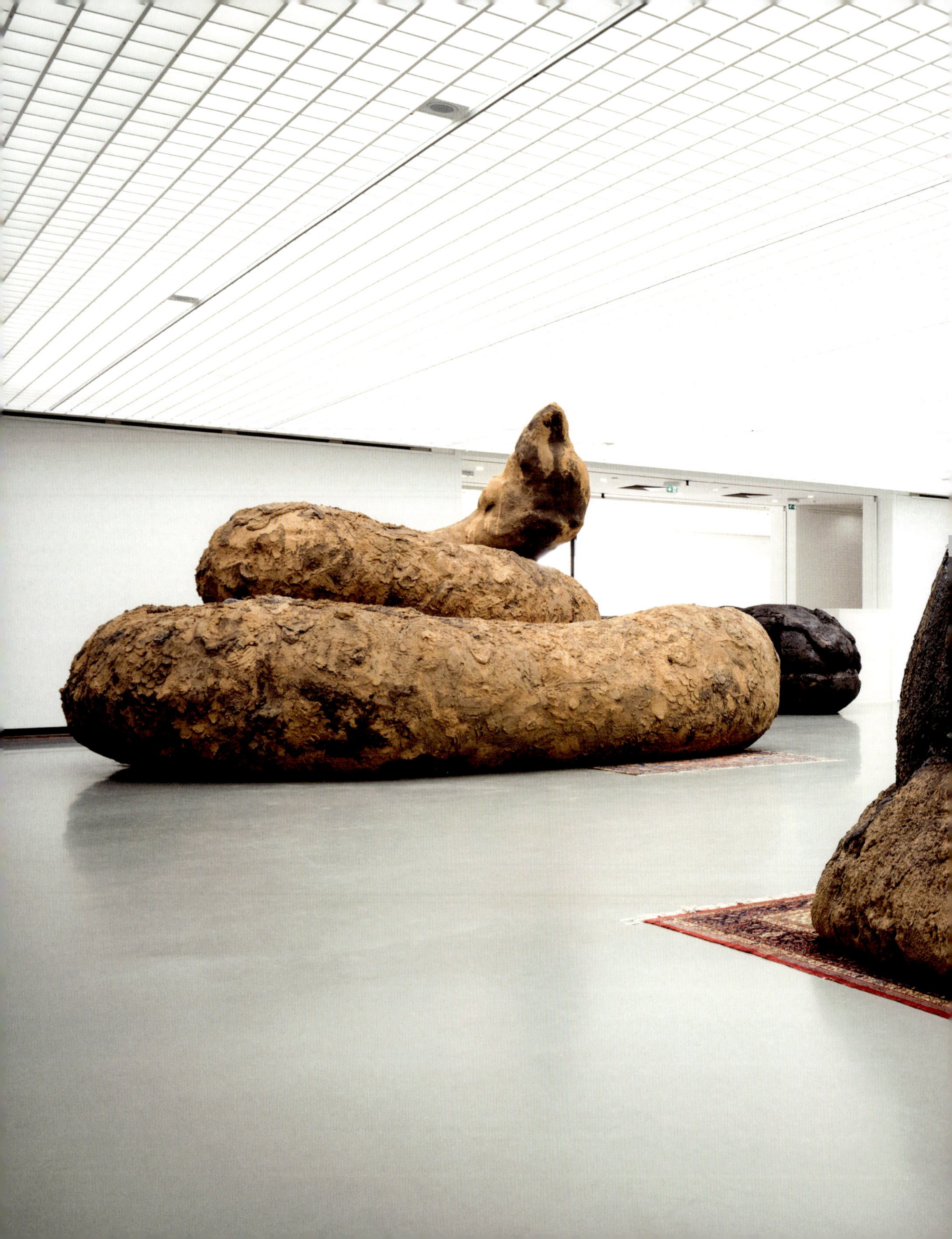

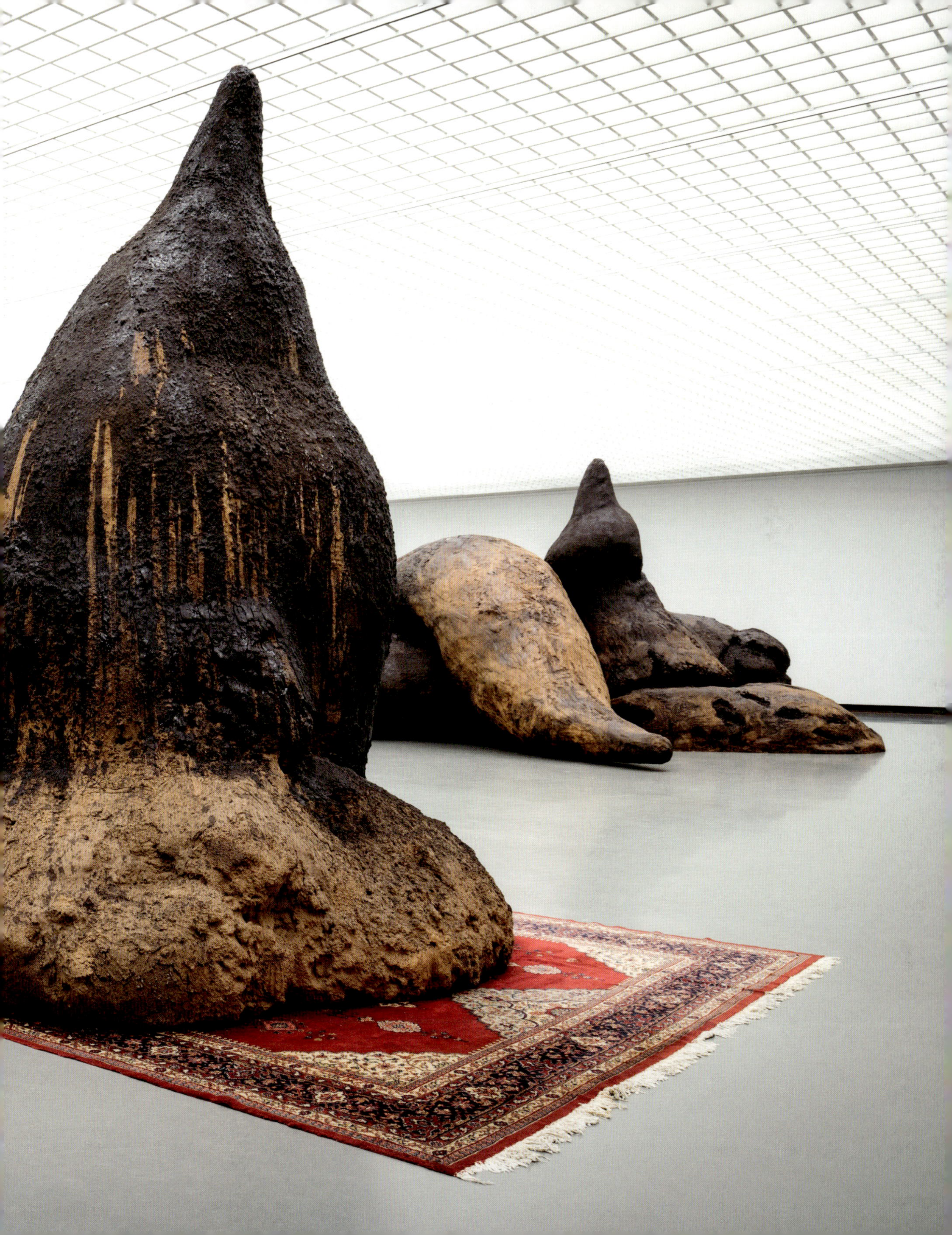

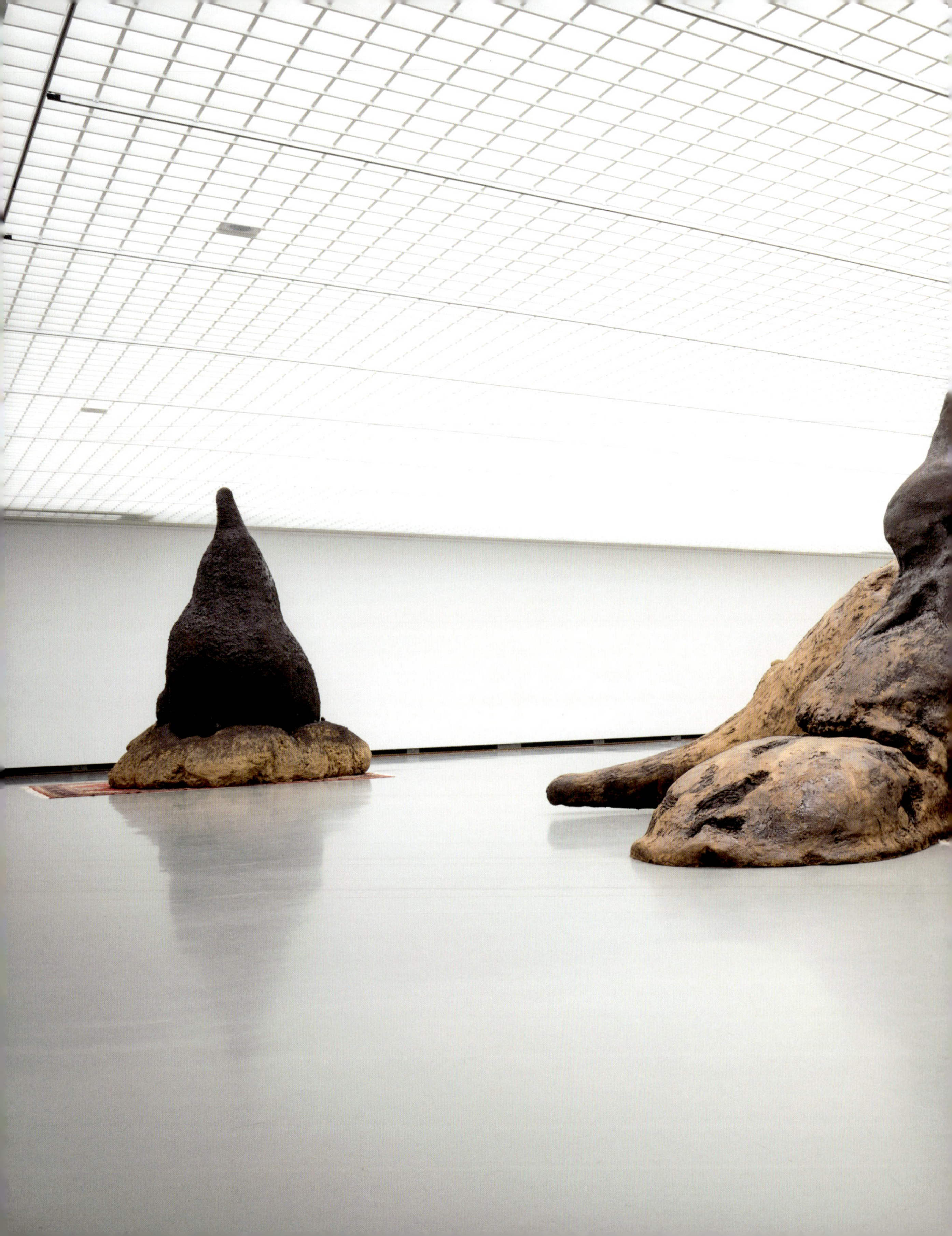

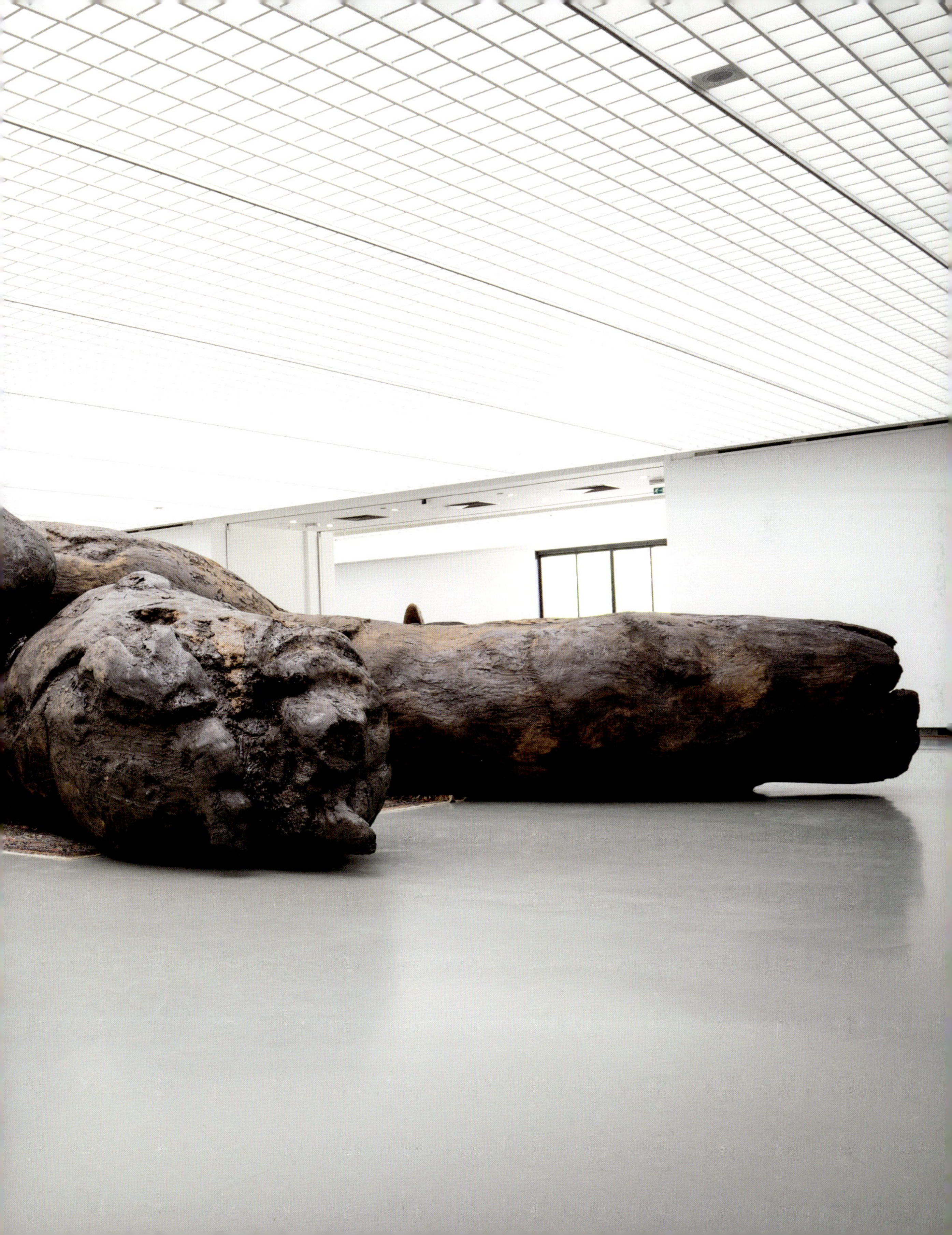

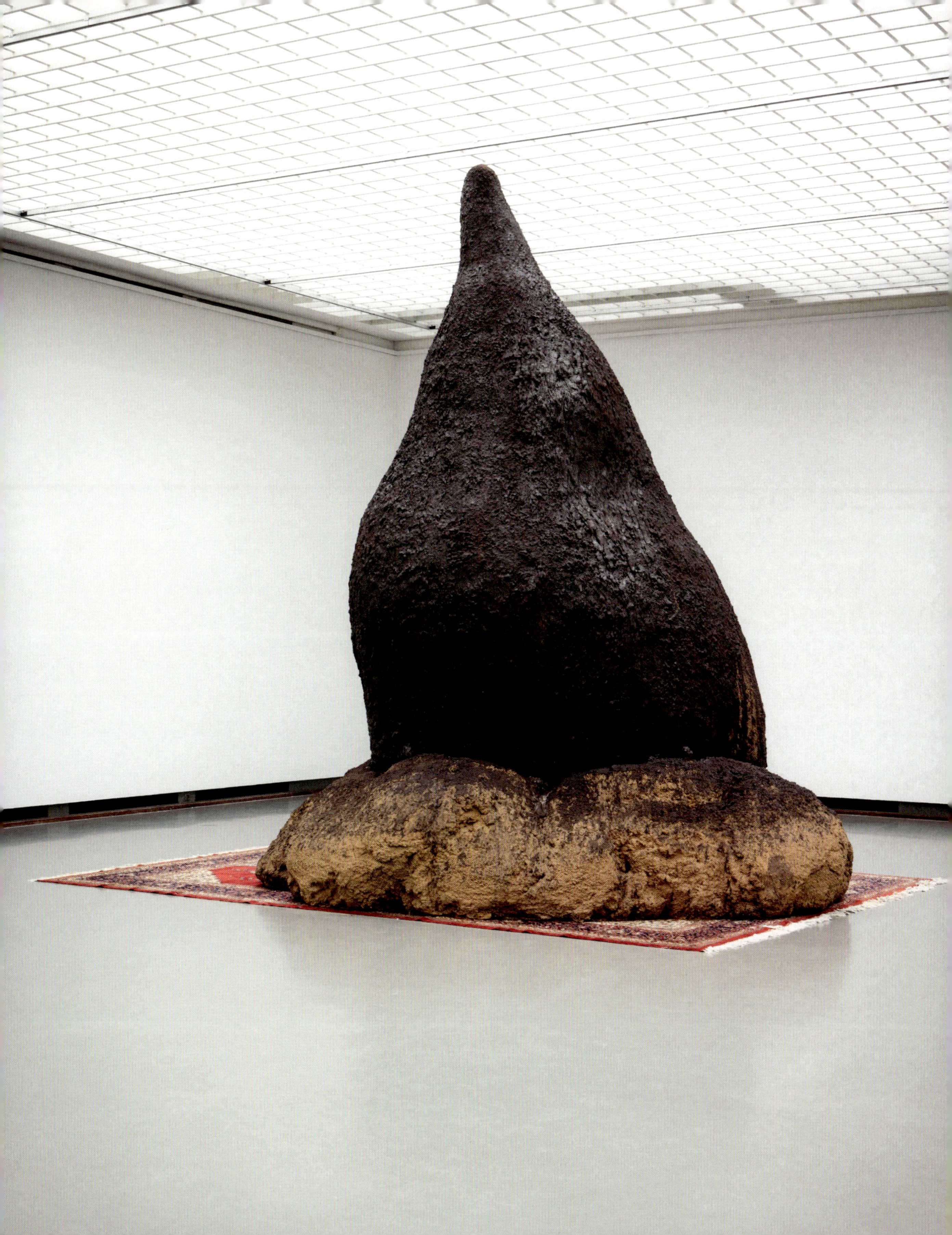

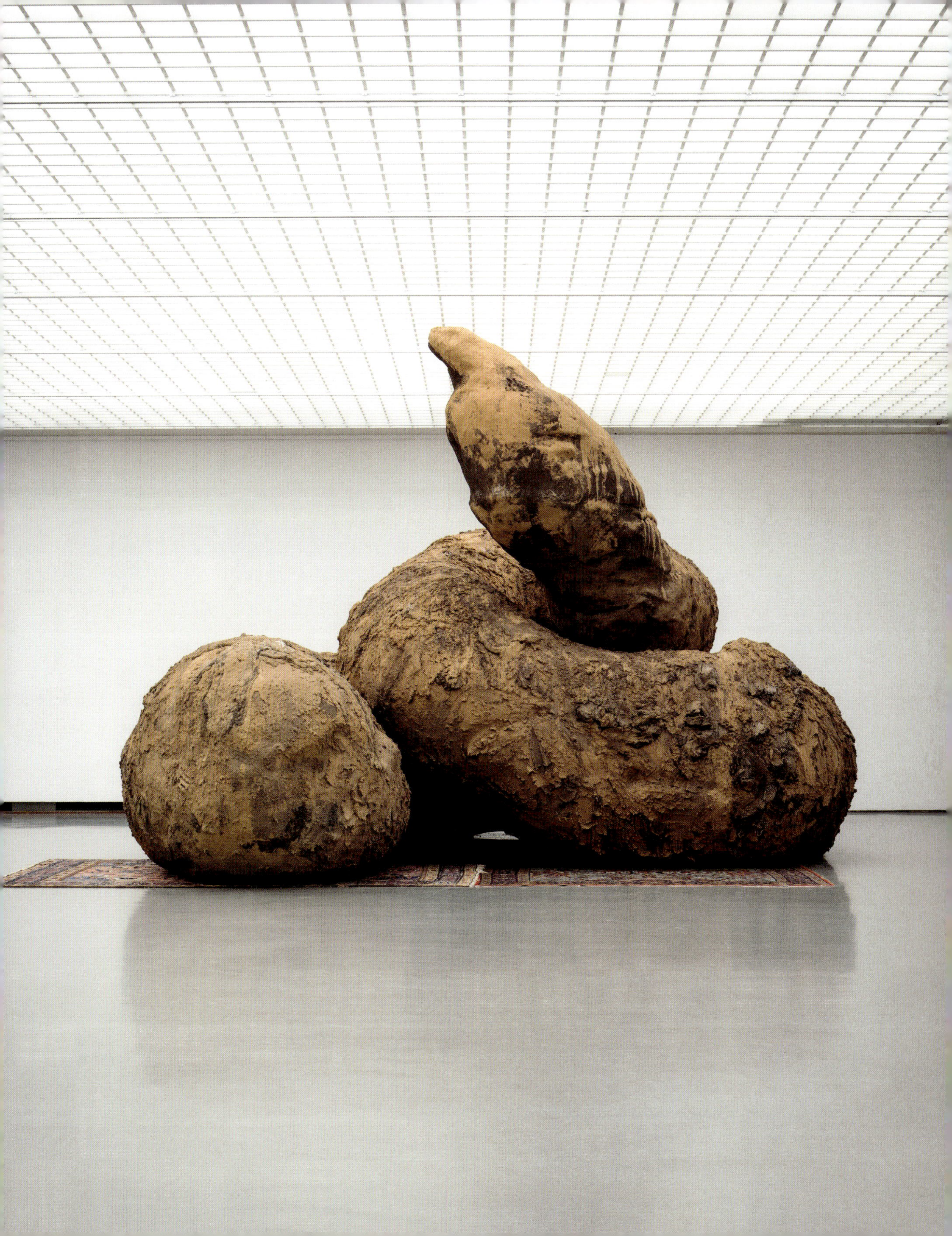

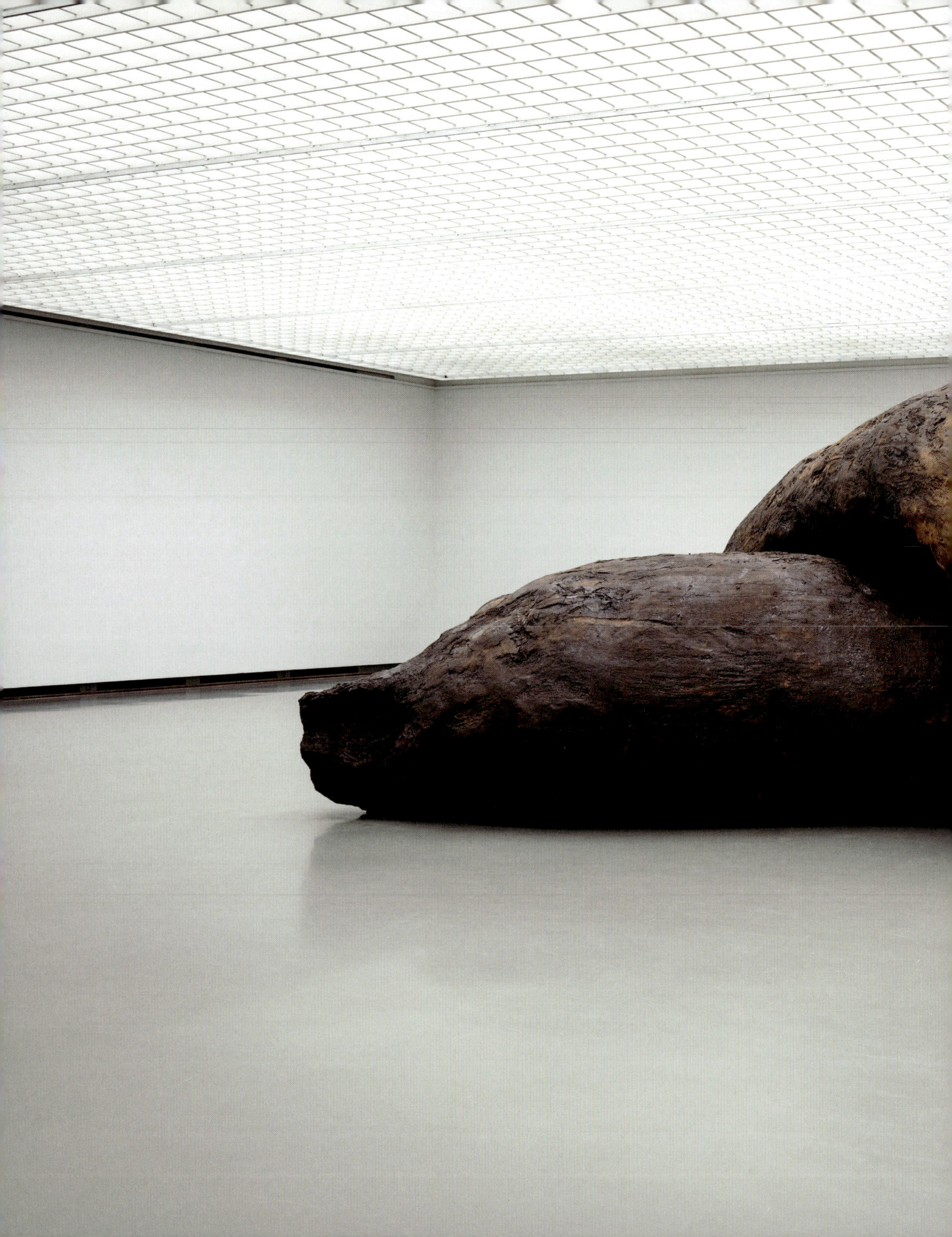

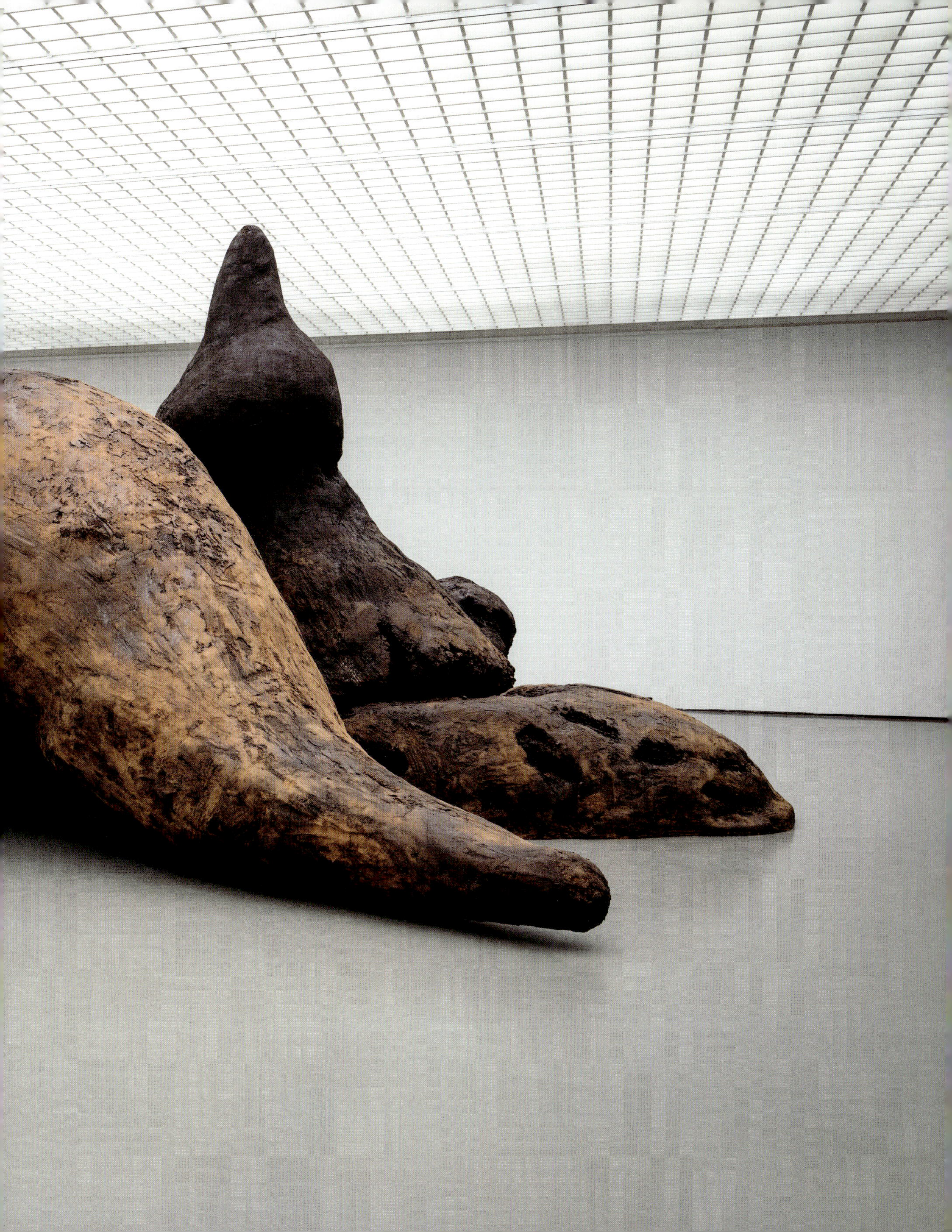

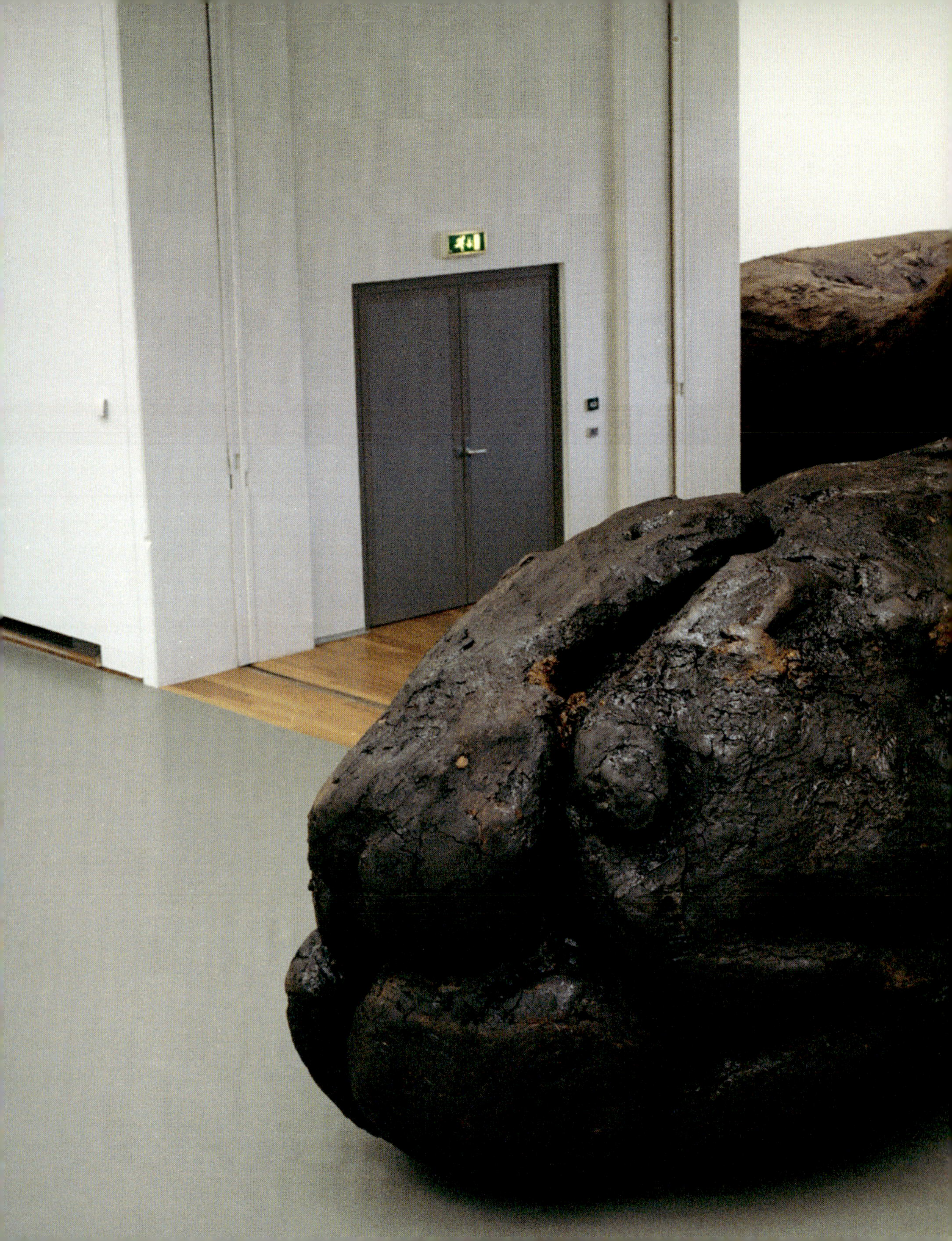

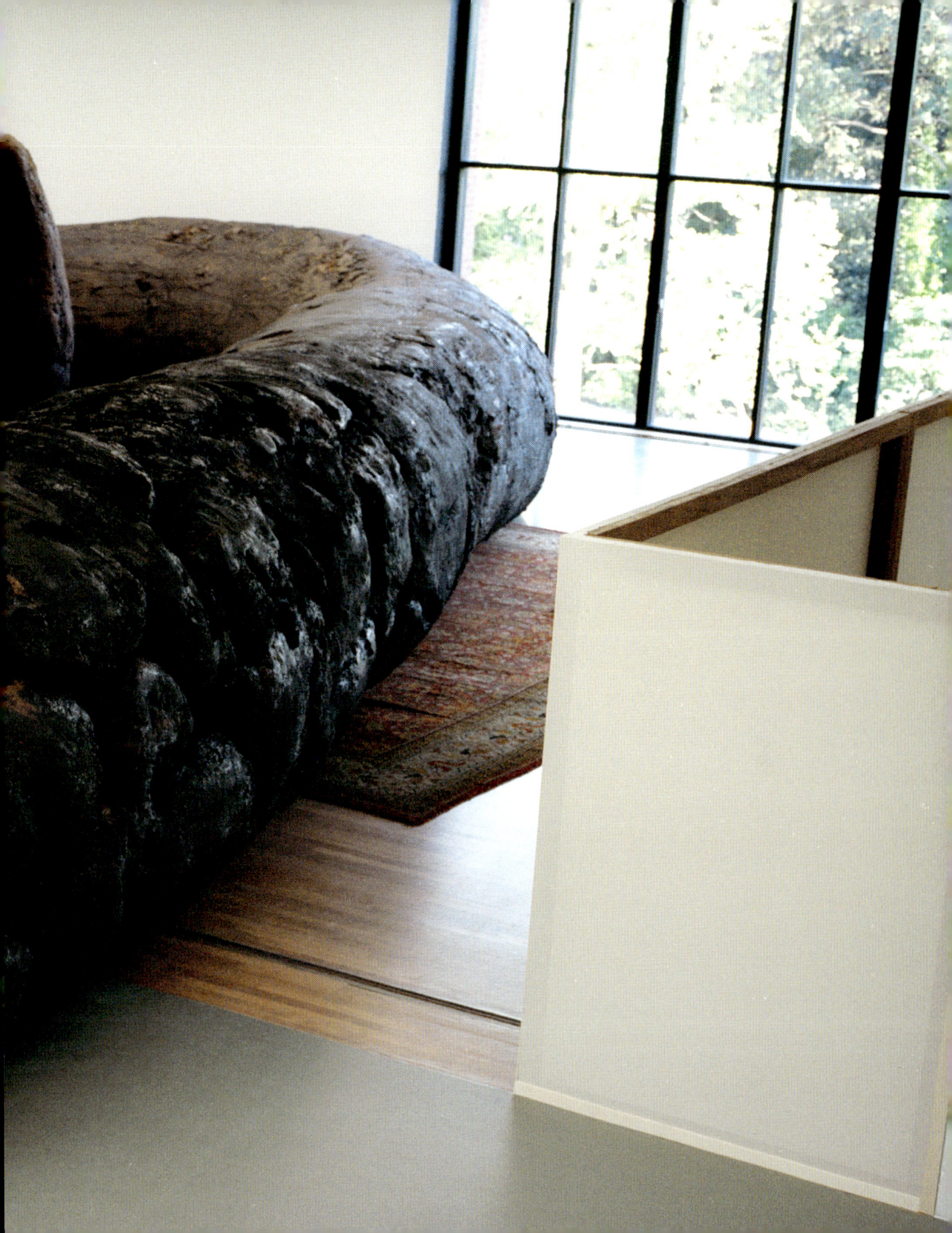

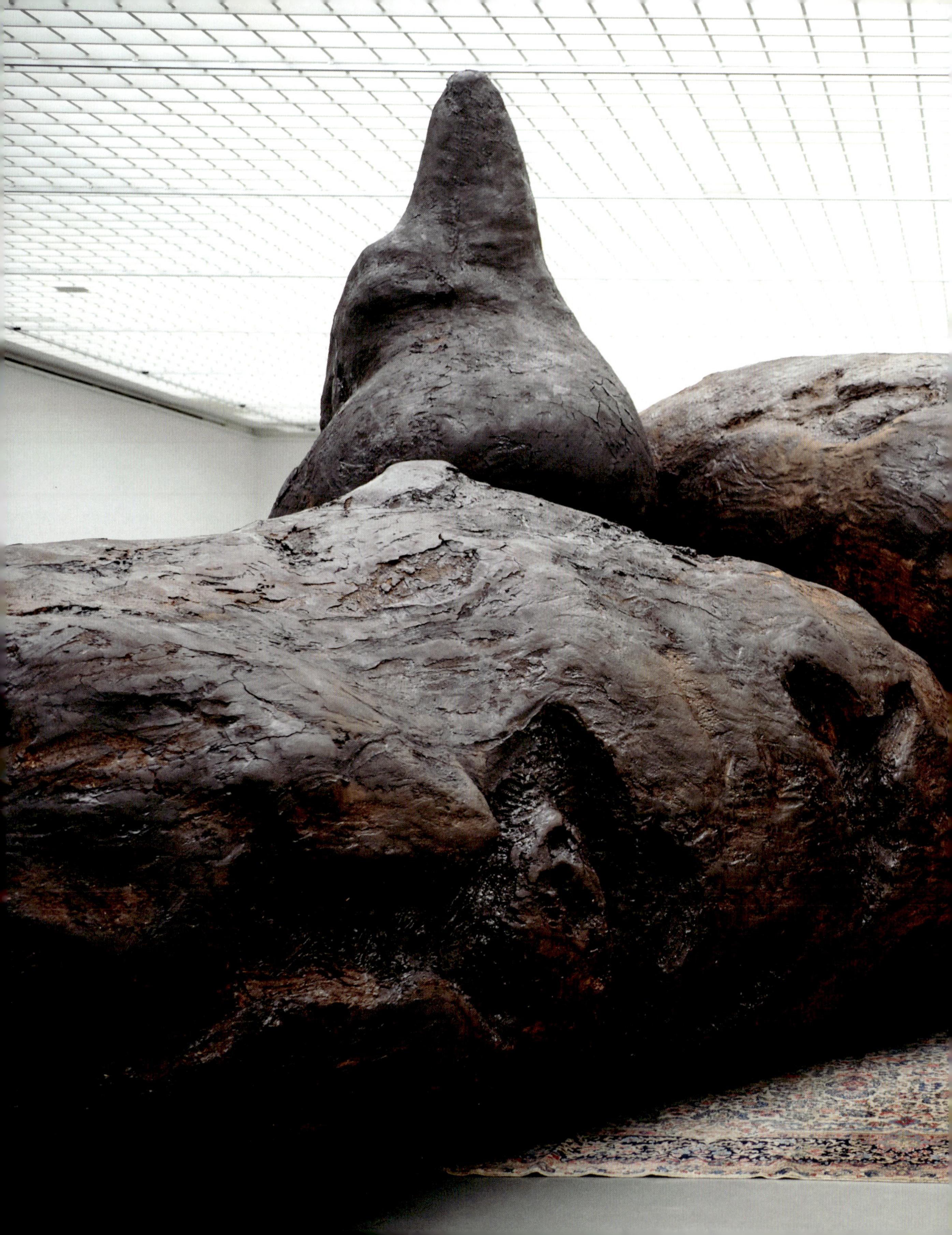

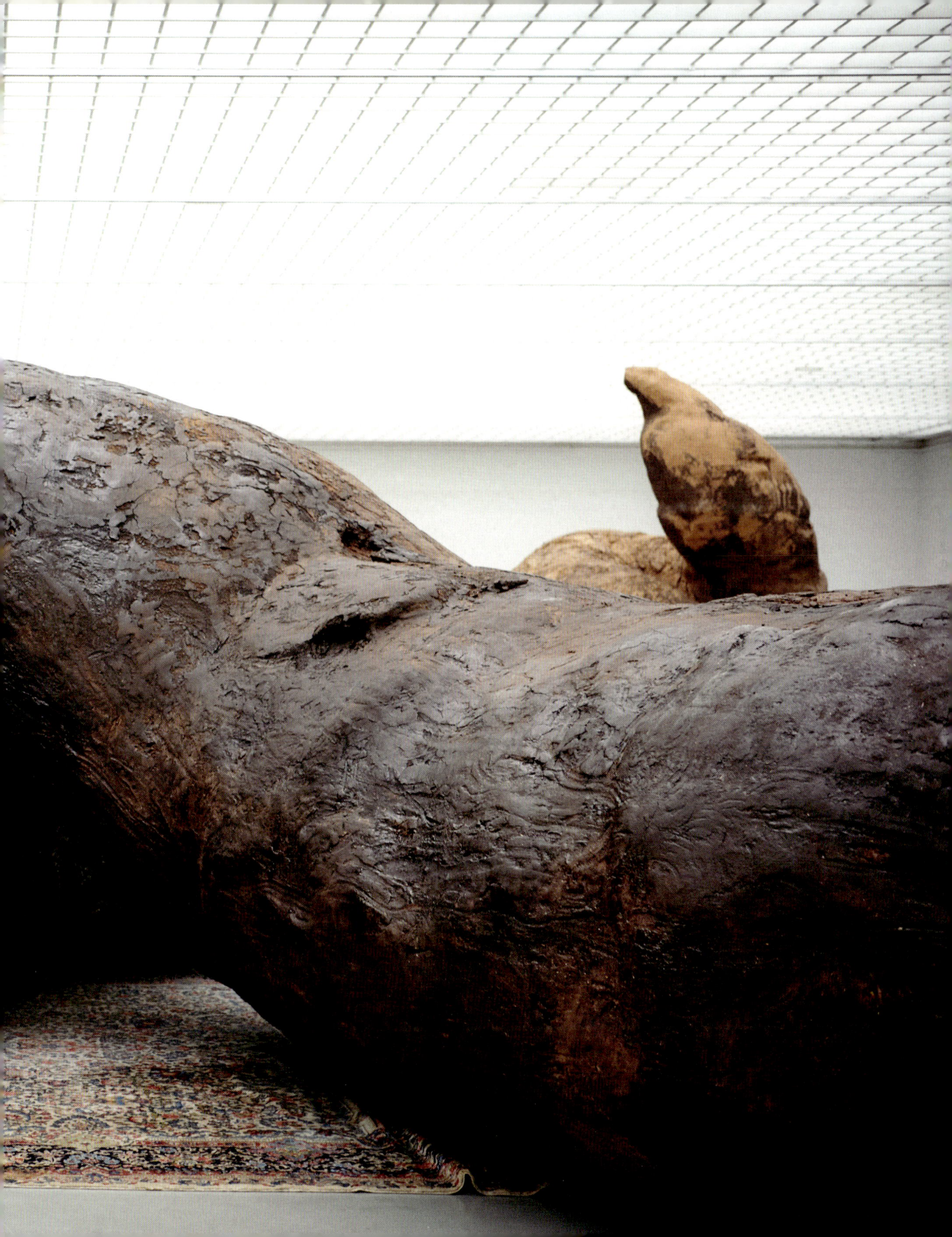

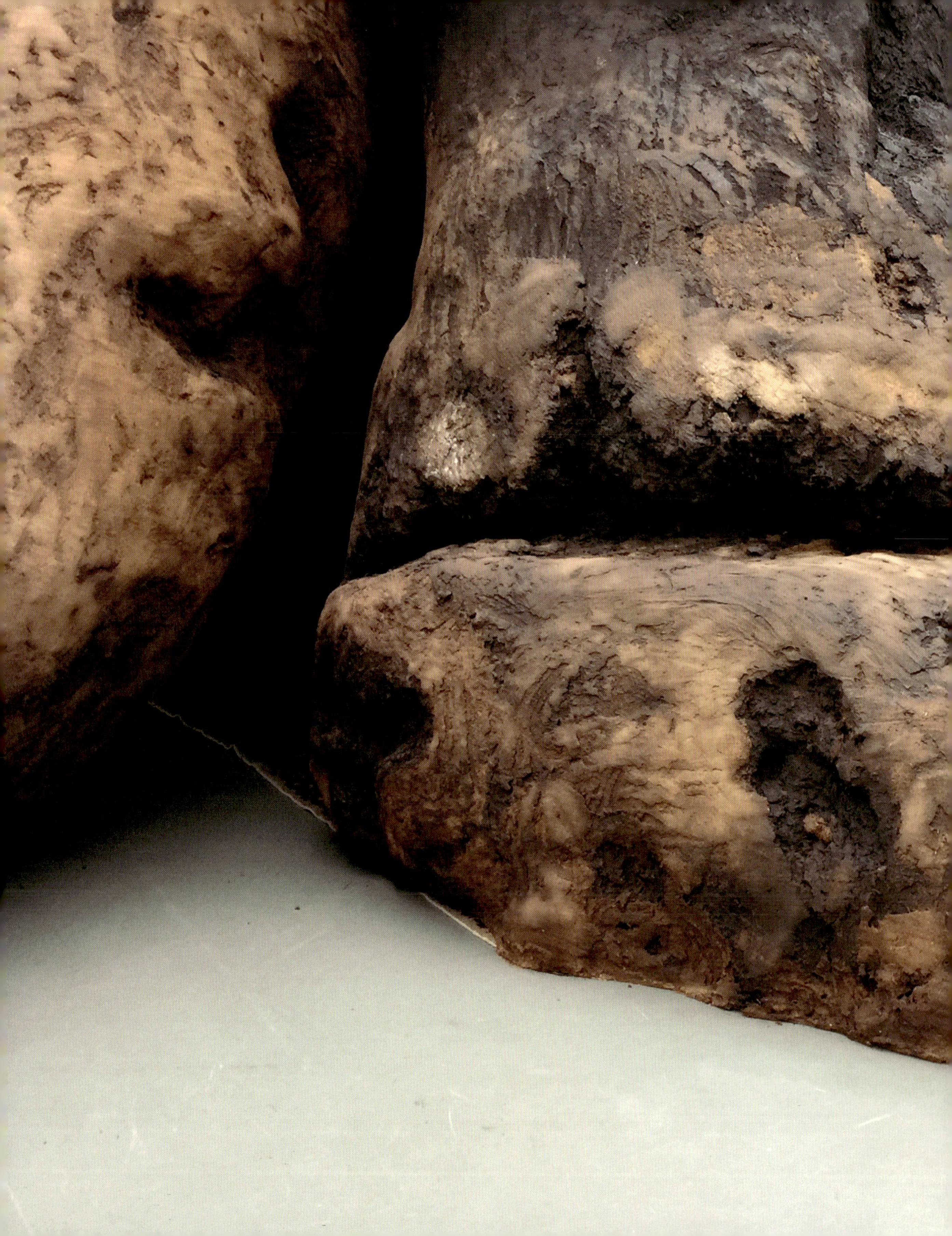

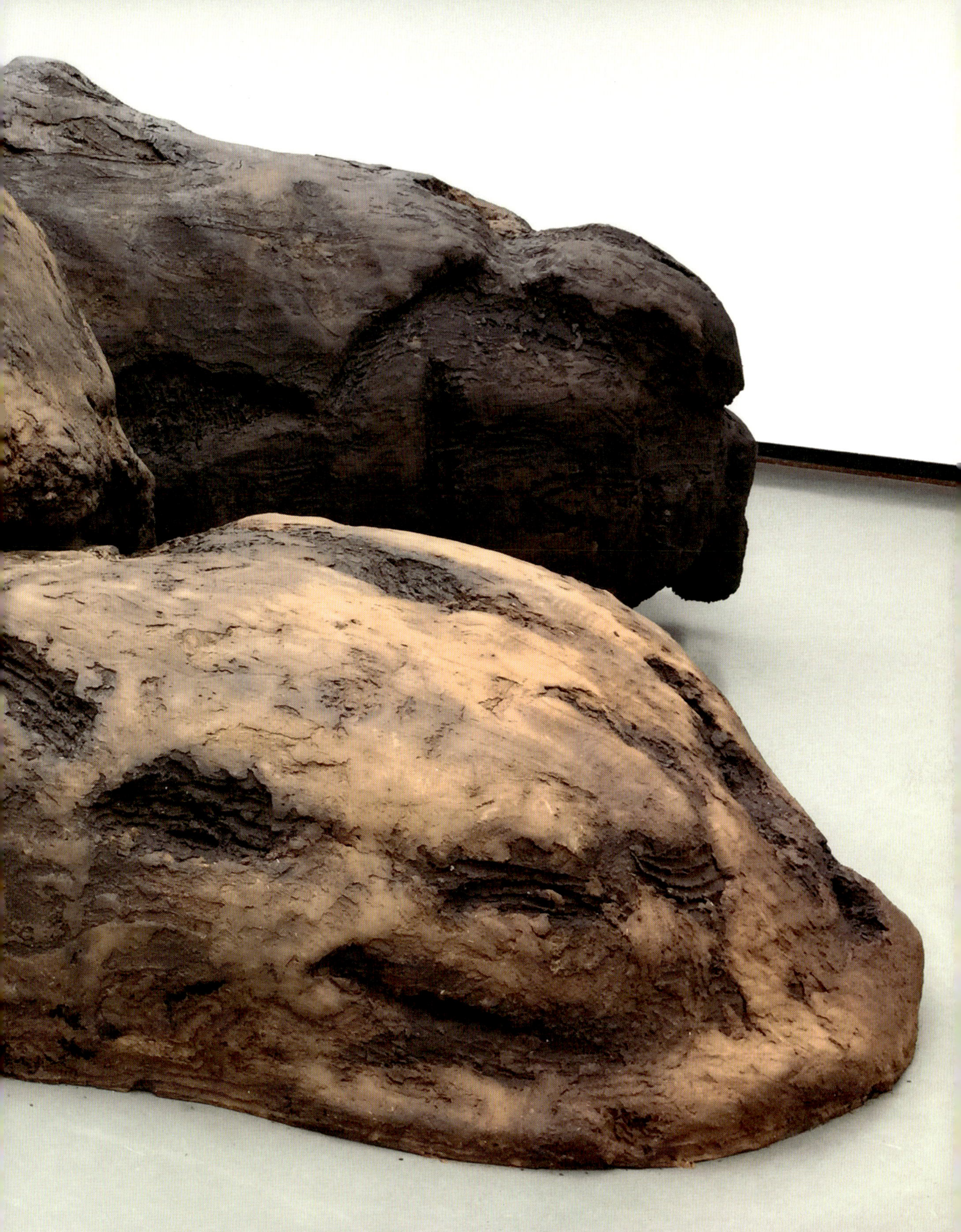

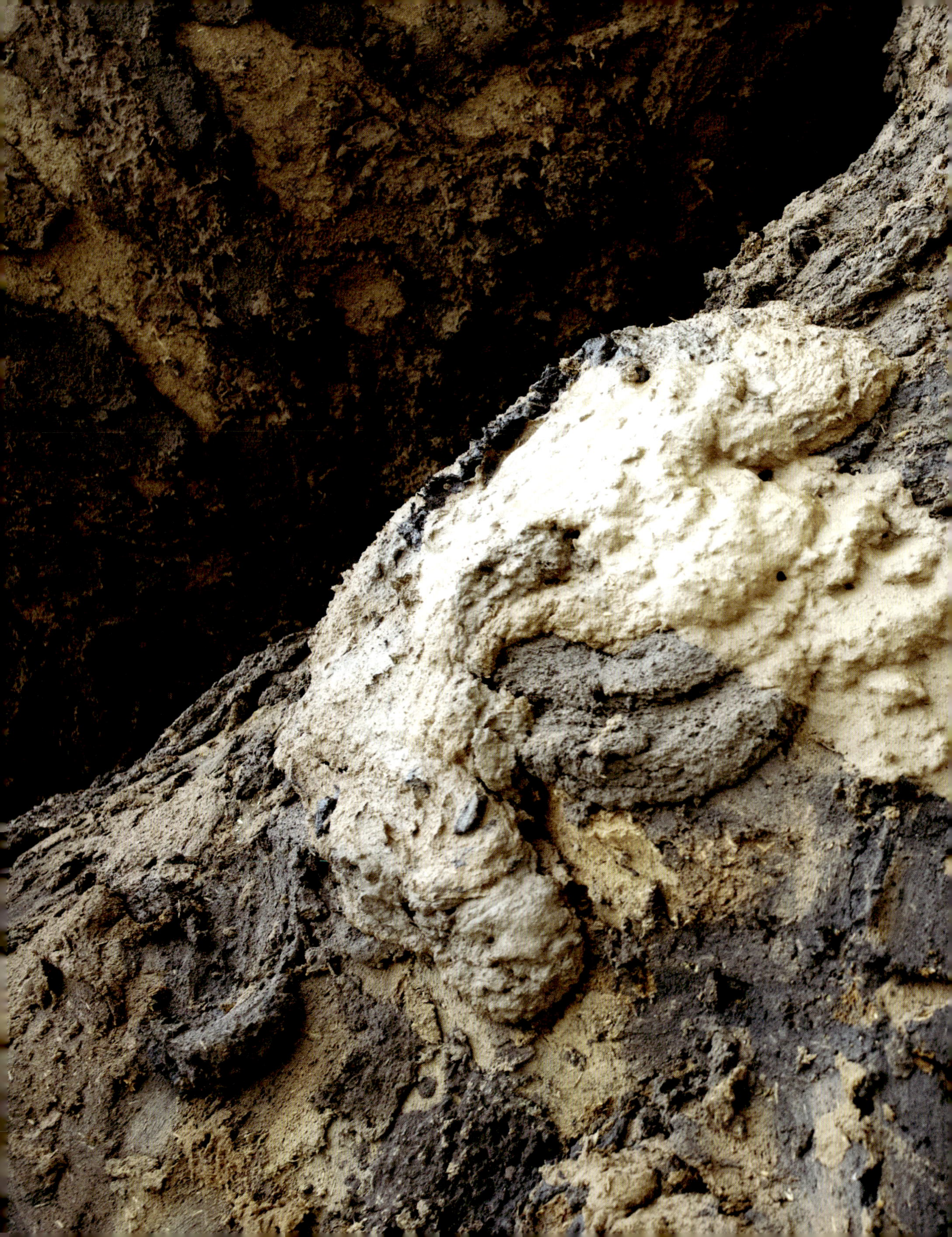

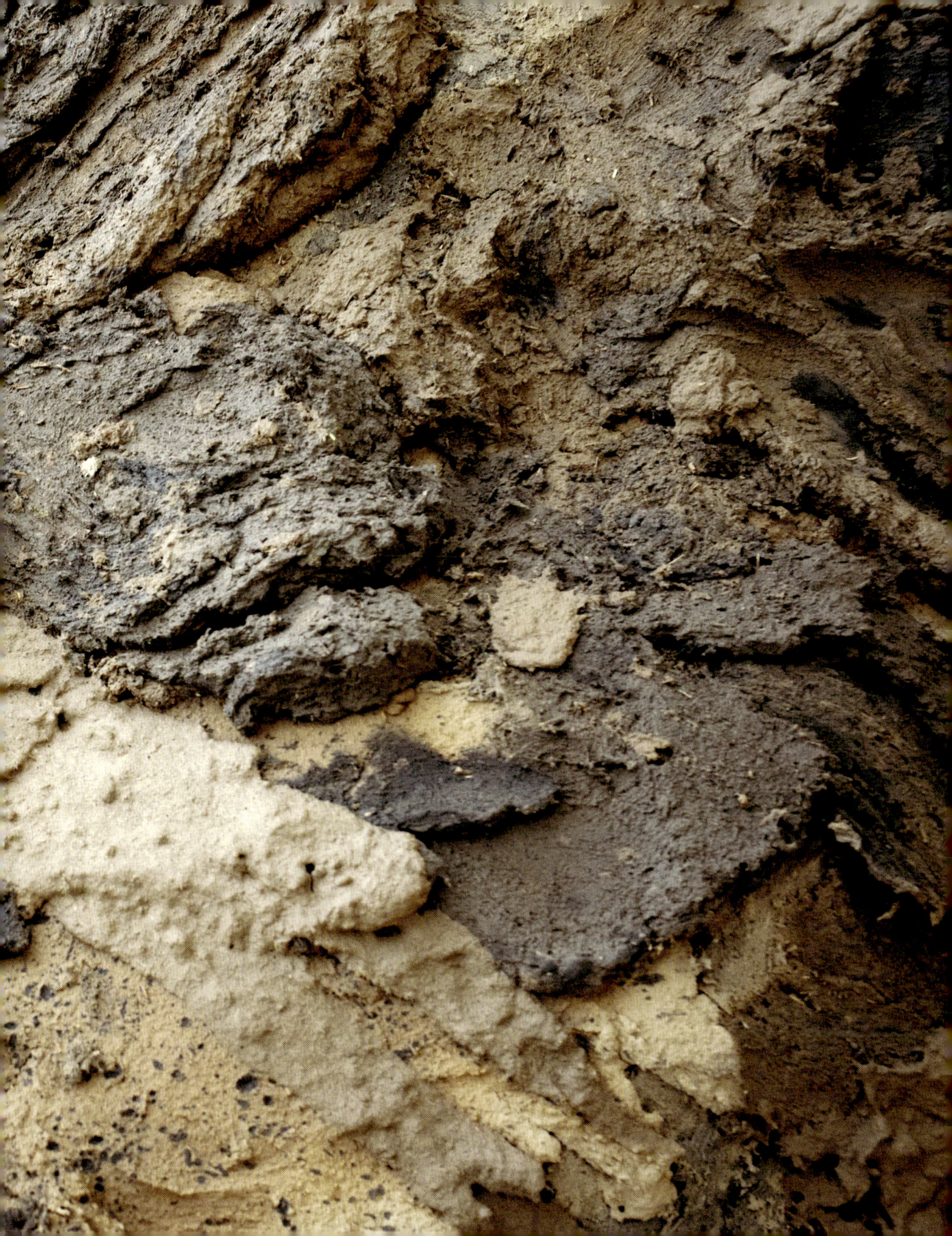

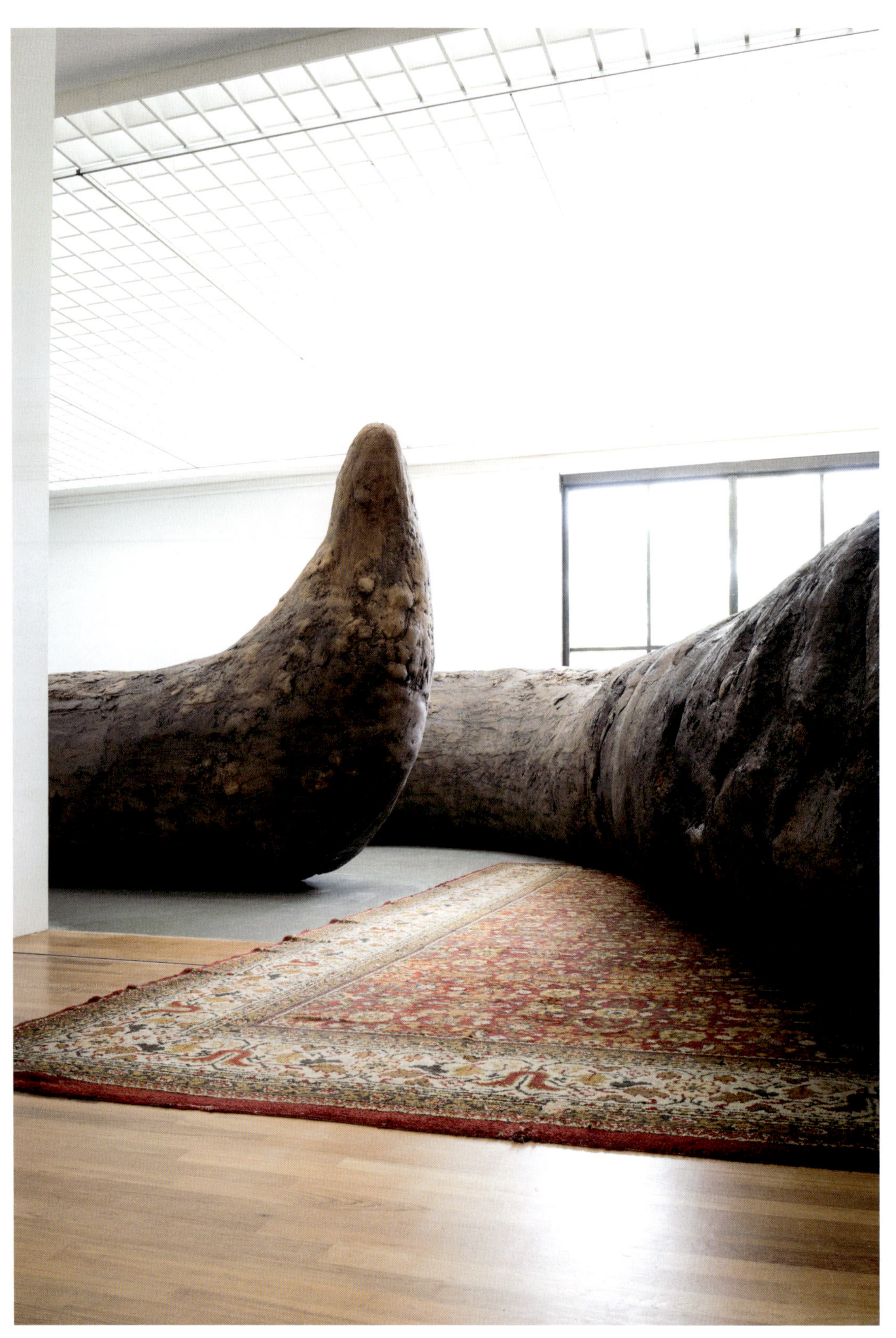

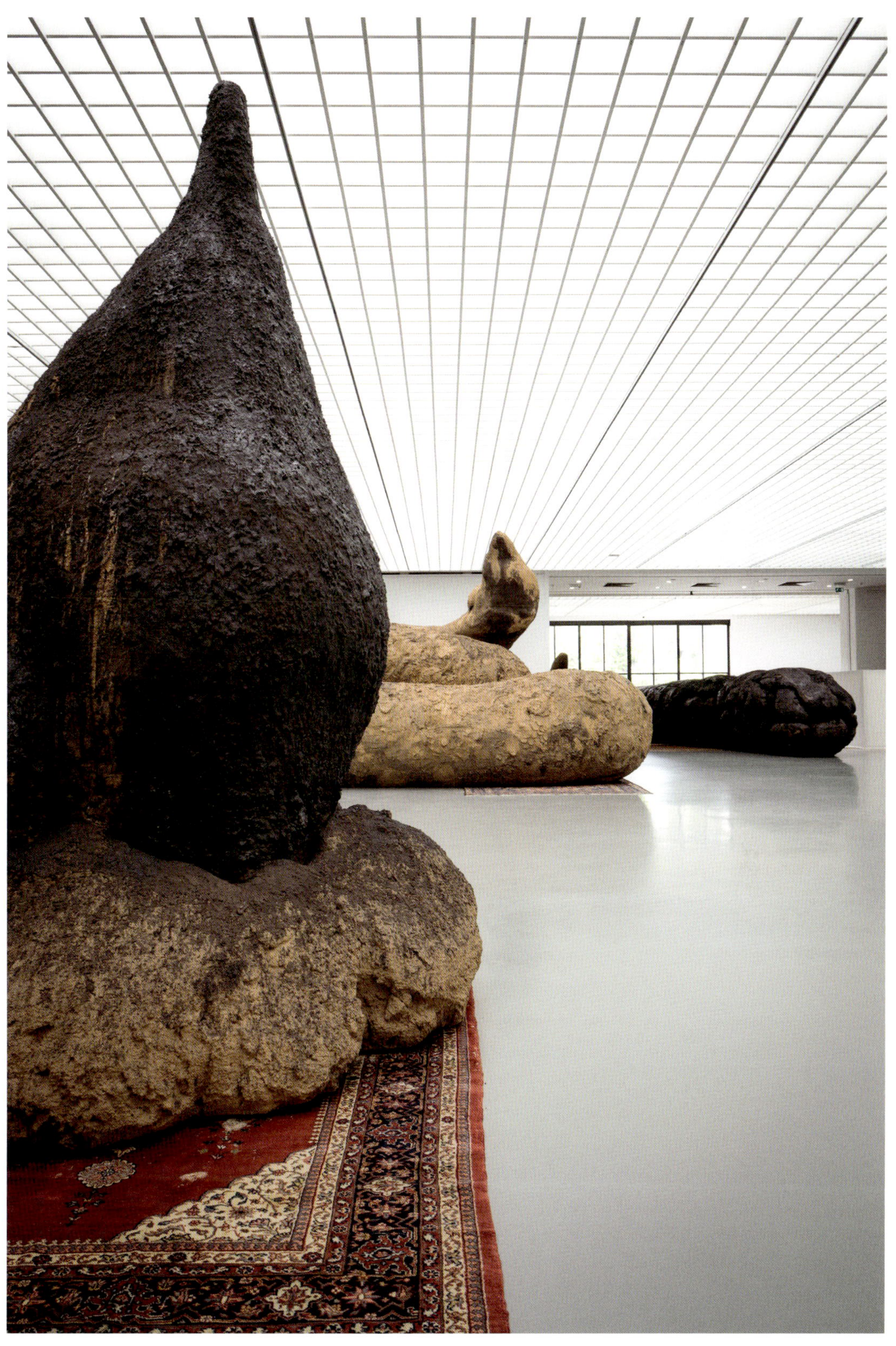

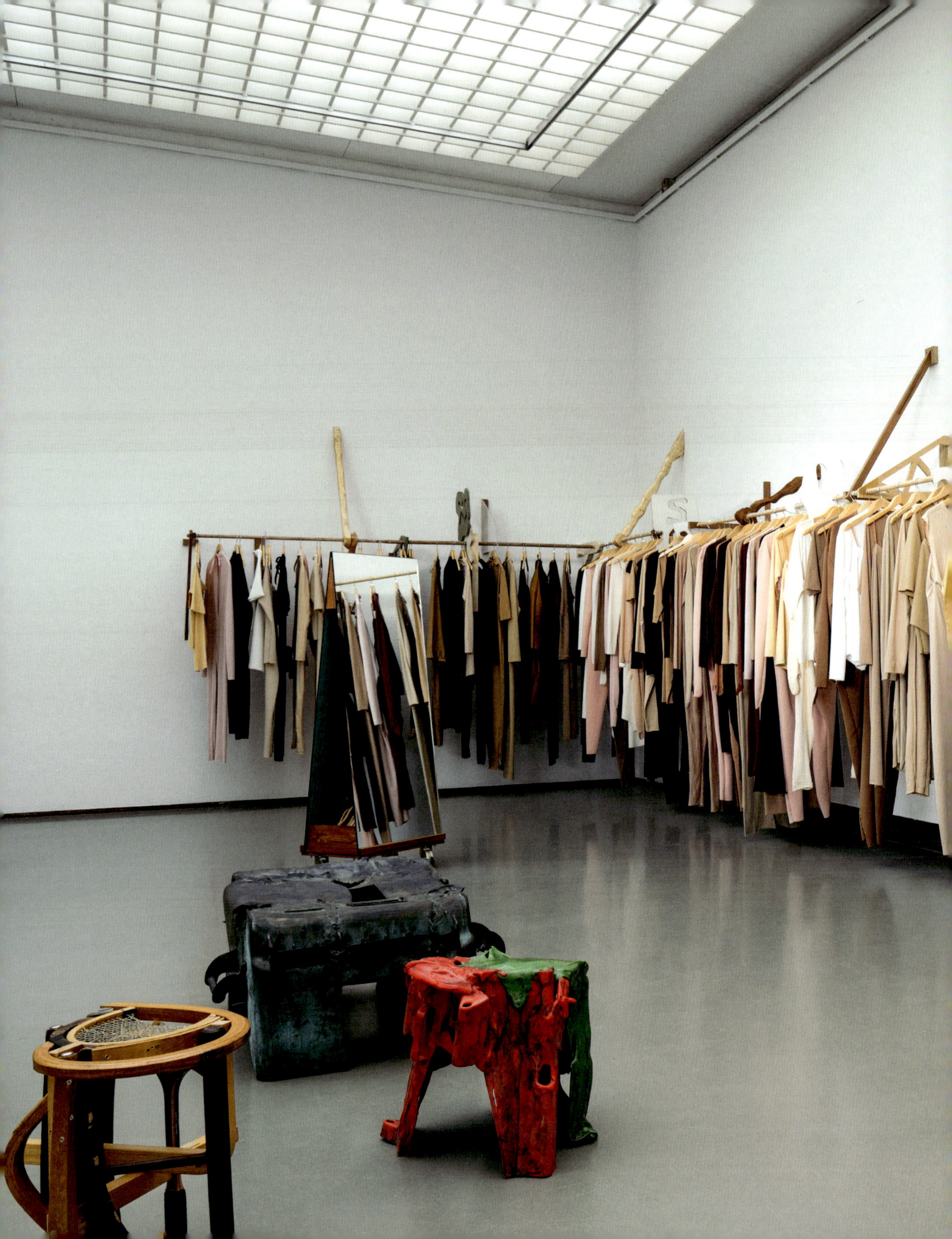

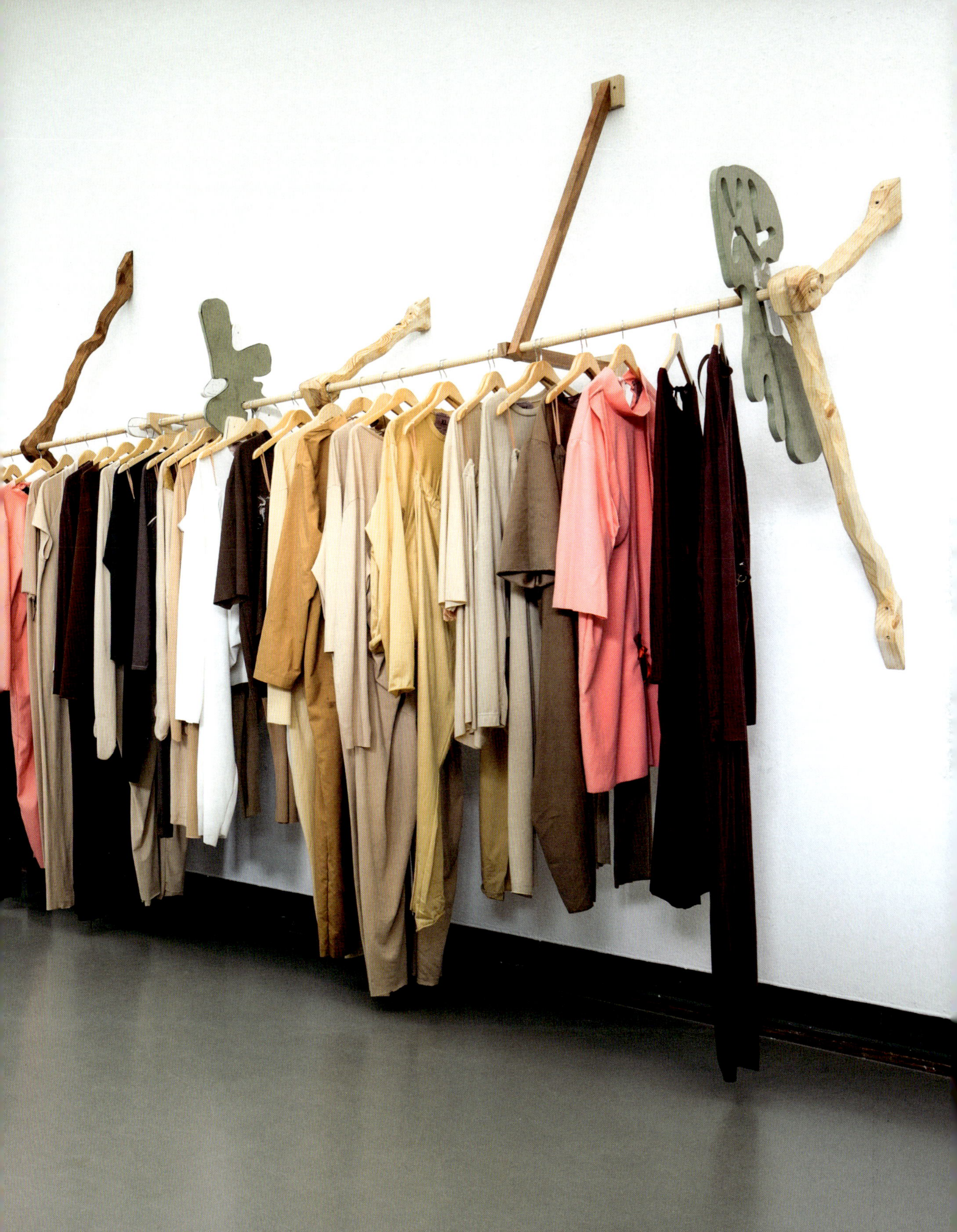

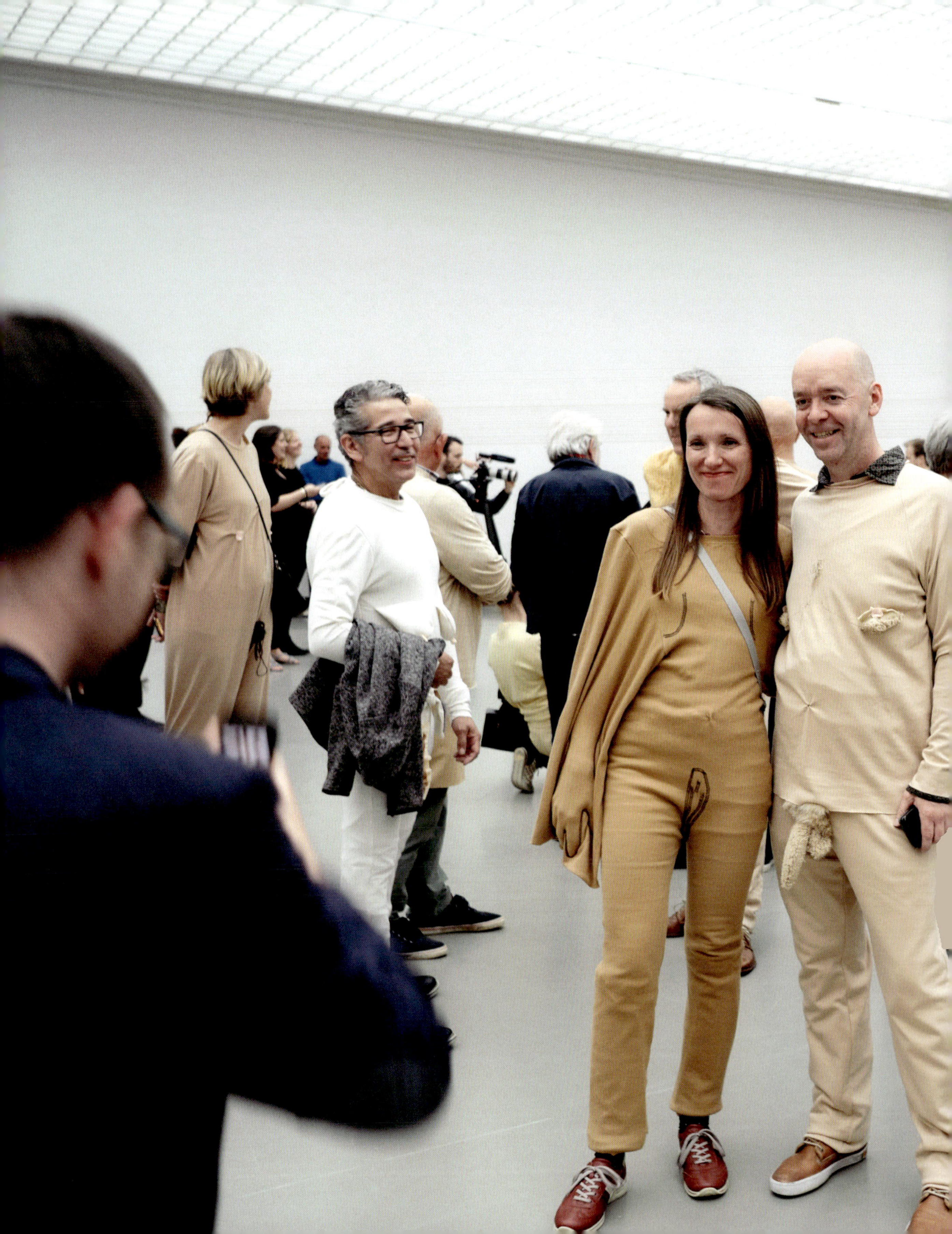

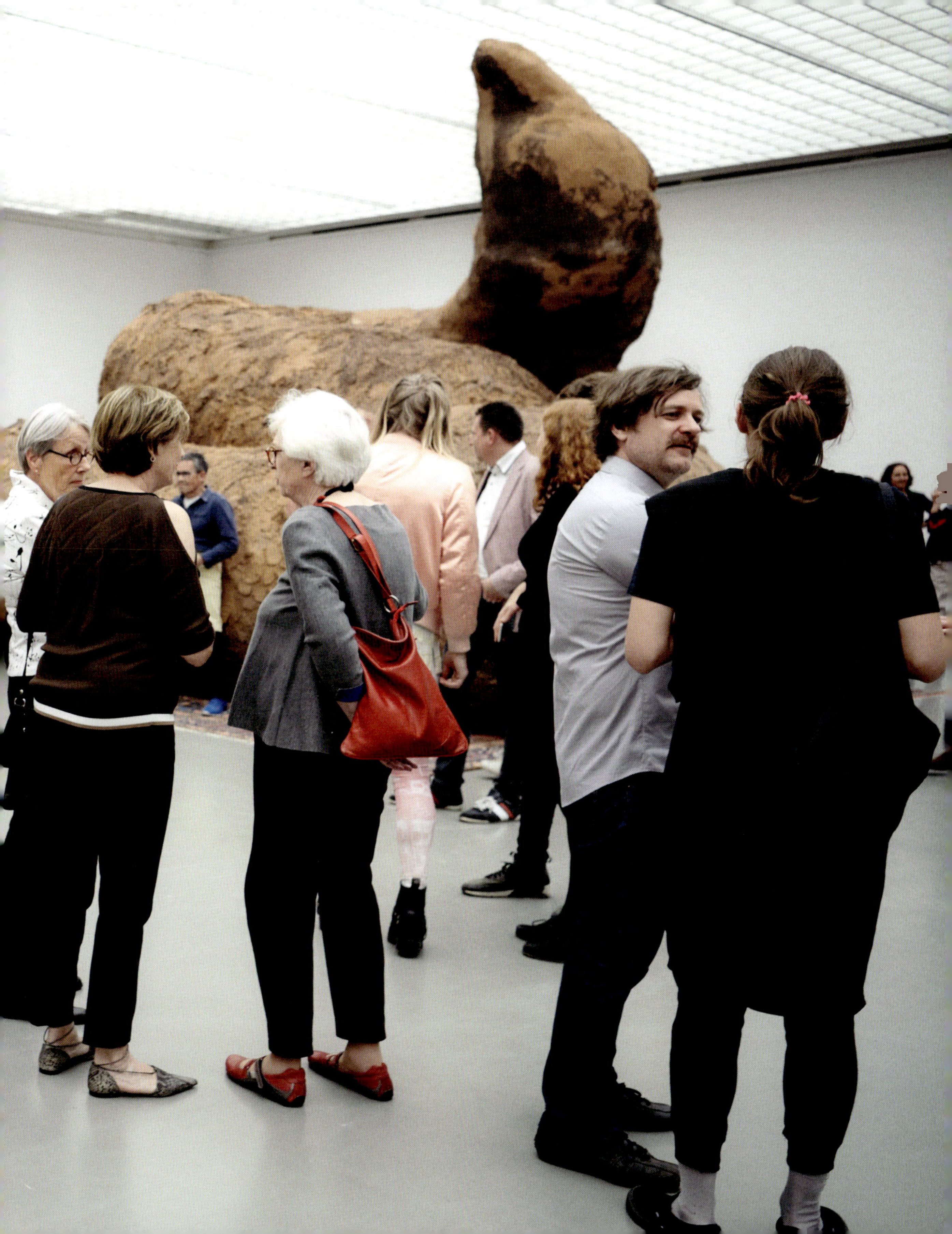

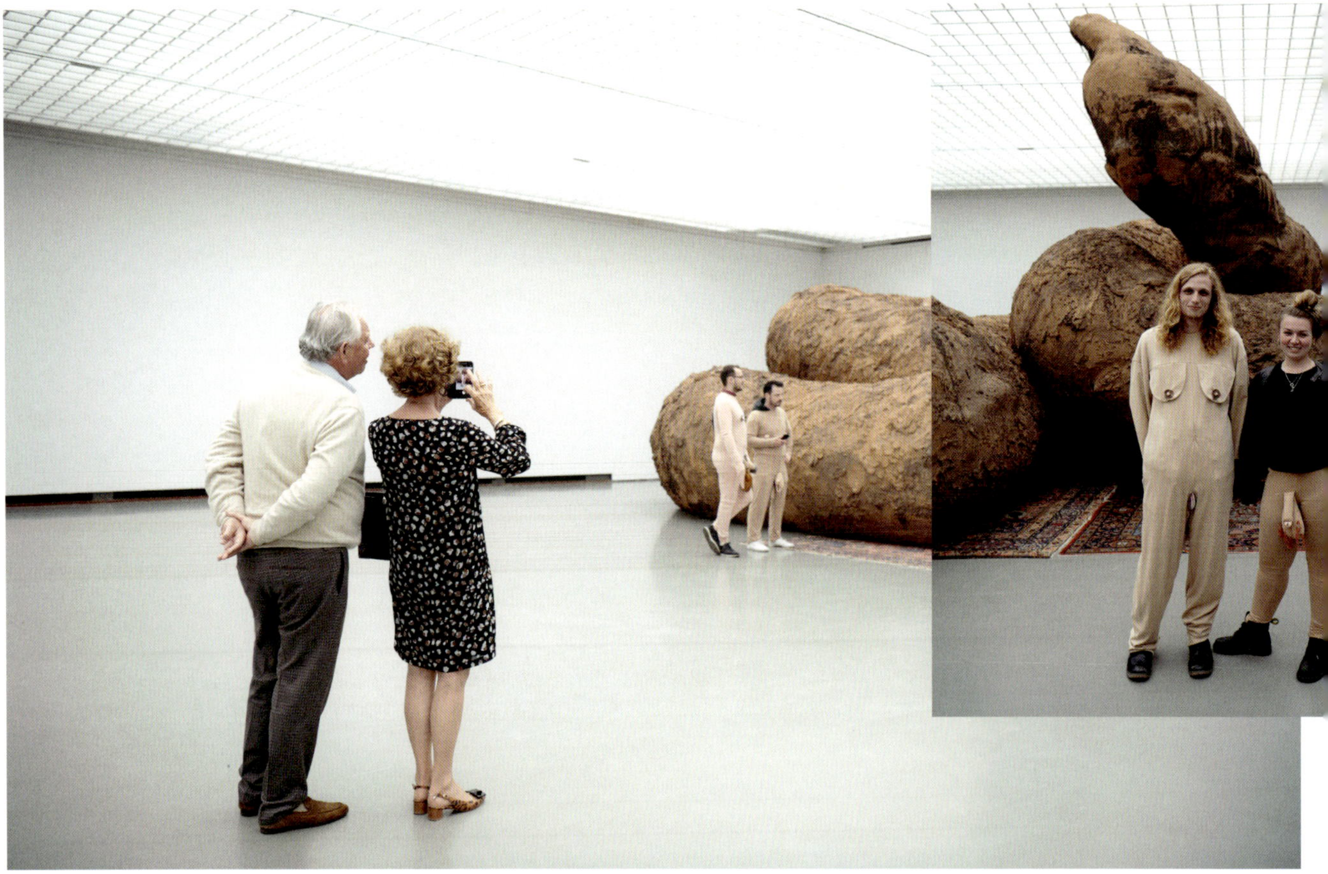

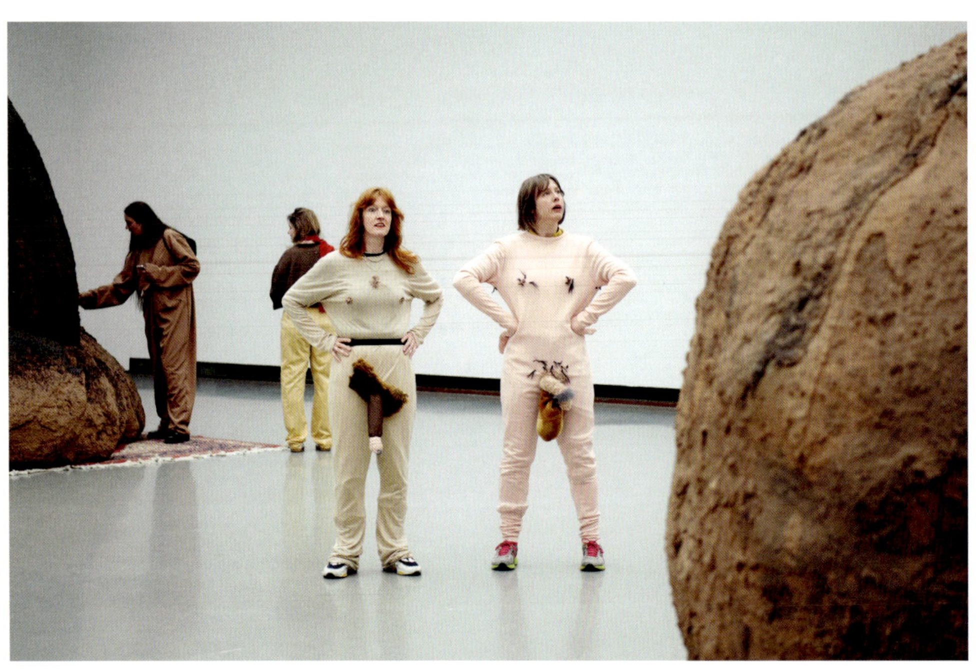

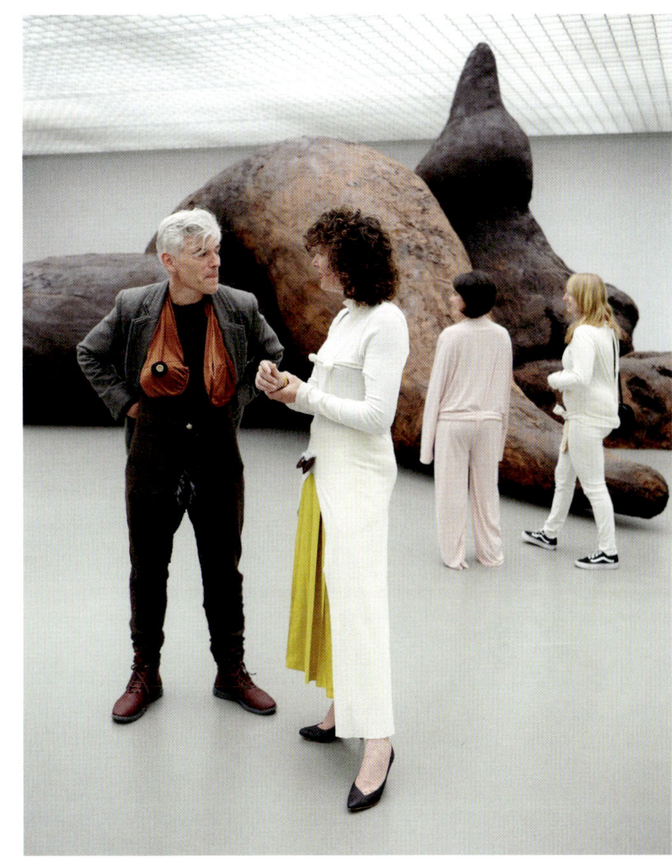

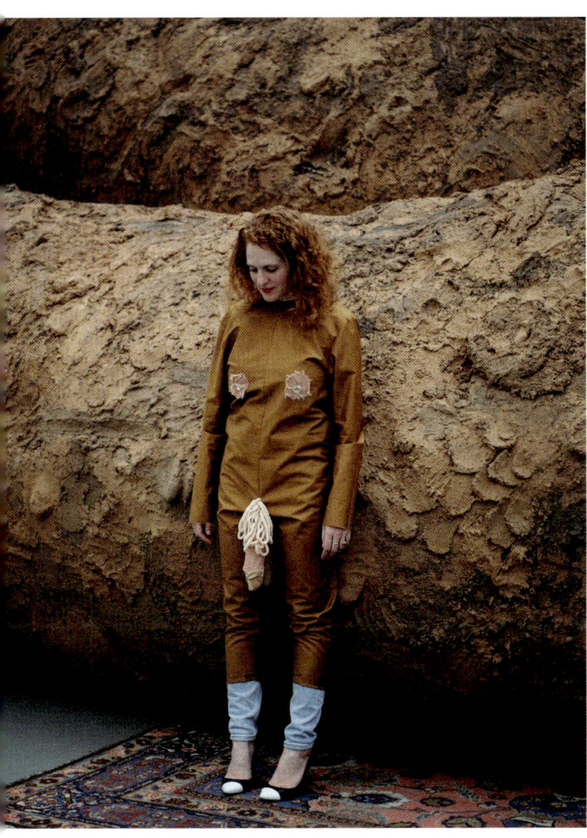

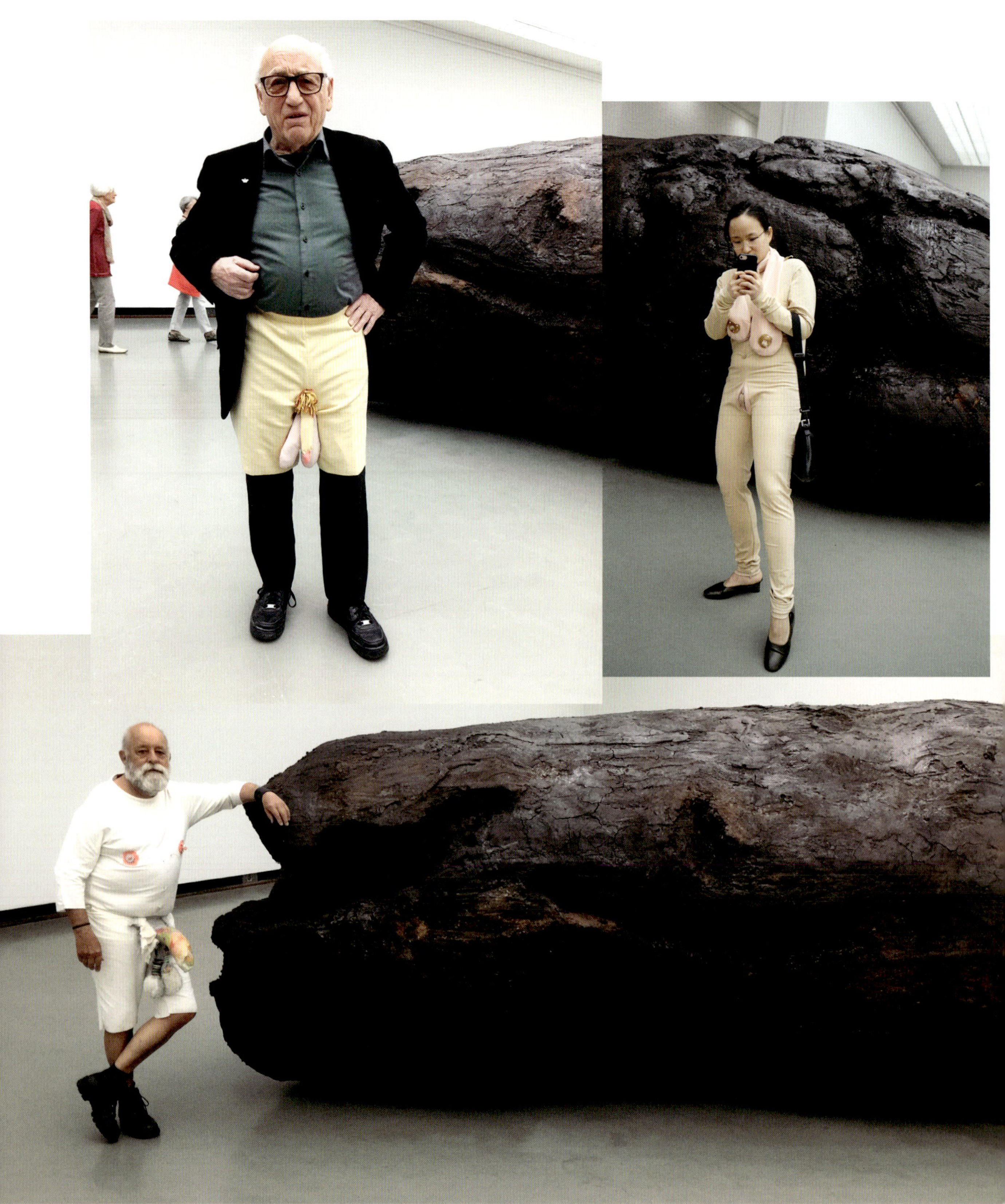

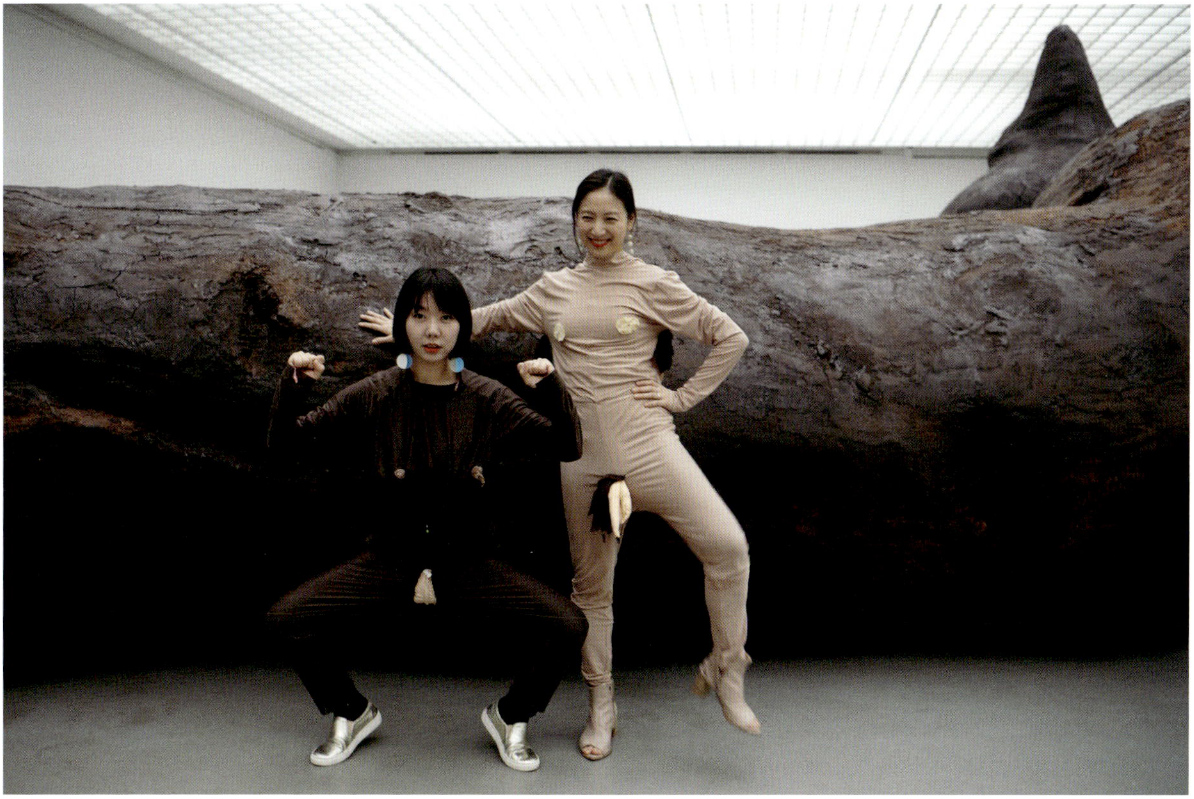

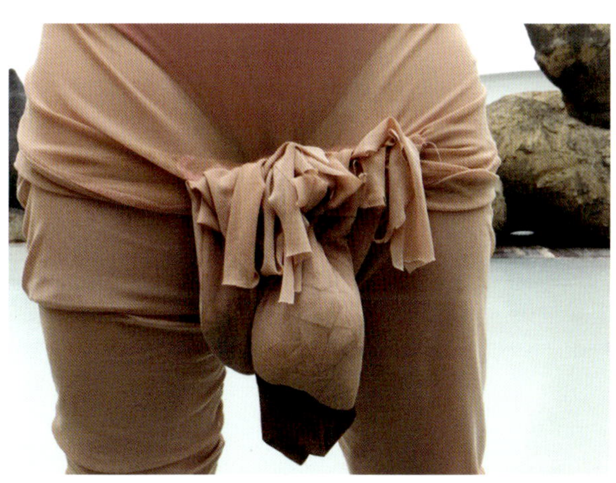

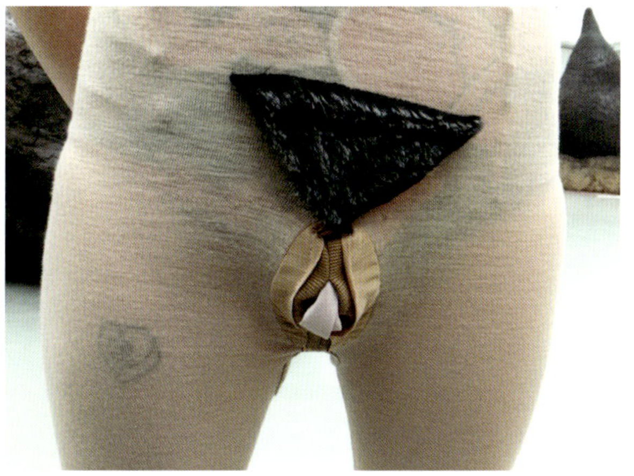

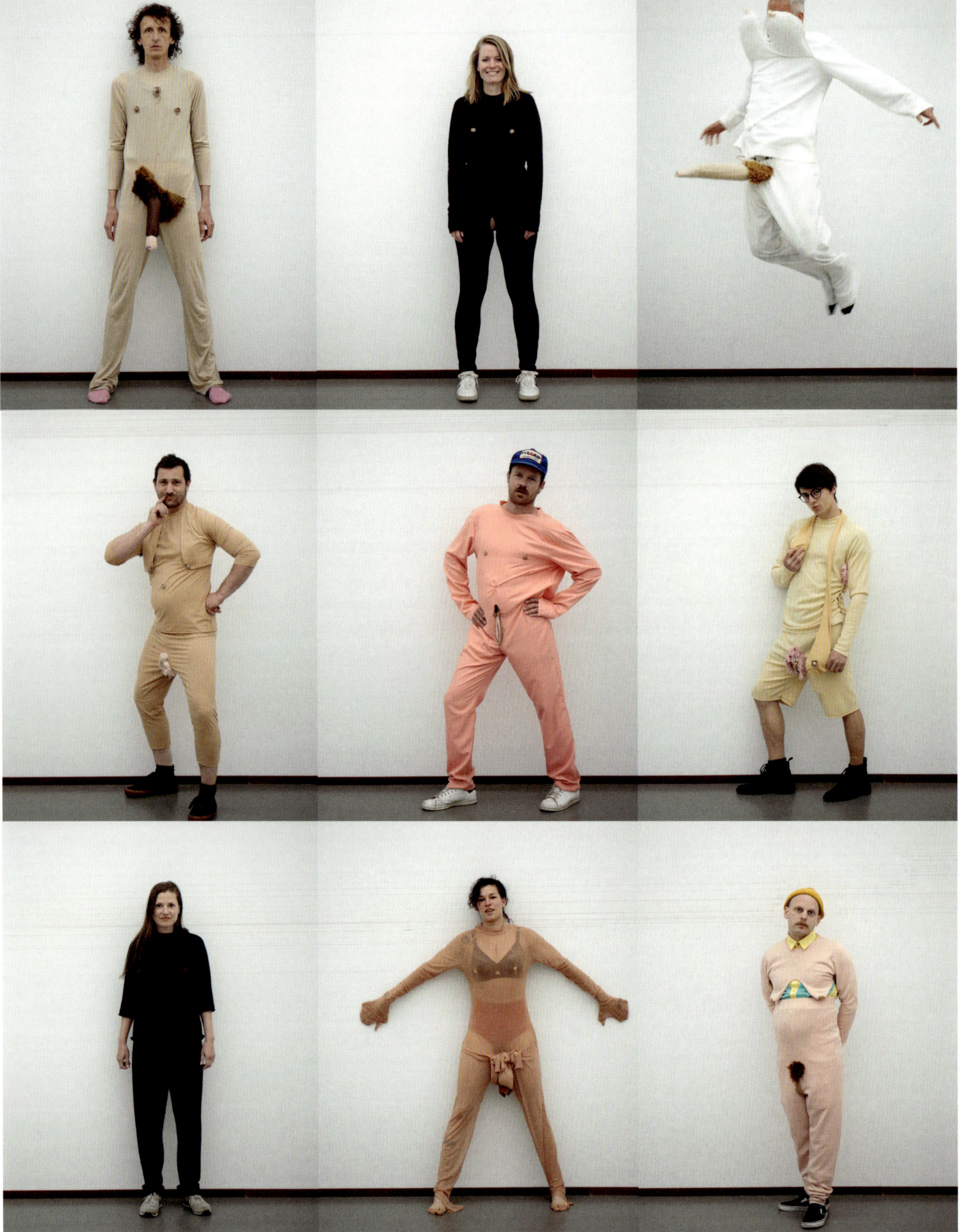

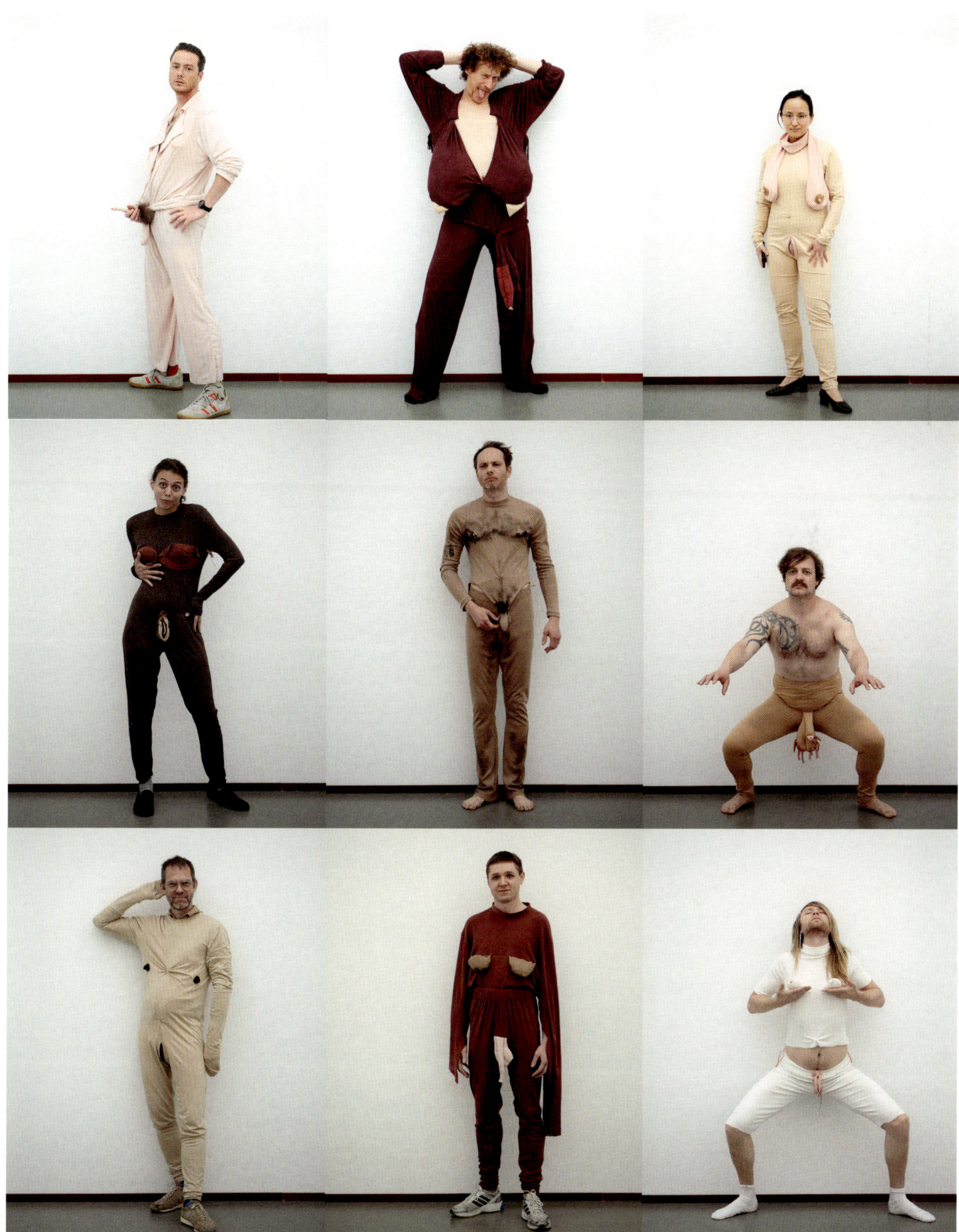

BACK TO THE TOILET
Revisiting the Shit Movement in Art: 1998 to 2018
Dieter Roelstraete

This text is based in part on an essay originally written for a Wim Delvoye catalogue published in 2002. A still earlier version of this essay was written in response to the premiere of Delvoye's Cloaca *installation (a machine replicating human excrement) in Antwerp in 2000, shortly before my first encounter with the work of Gelatin. I have omitted all but one reference to Delvoye's work and repurposed my argument in strongly condensed form—no more "semantic diarrhea" as in the original—for Gelatin's sake.*

Sometime in the early nineties, feeling my way around the minefield of theorizations of the postmodern—the subject of my thesis research in philosophy at the time—I came across a well-packaged treatise by the American art critic Neville Wakefield, seductively titled *Postmodernism: The Twilight of the Real.* Wakefield's diagnosis of the postmodern condition as one characterized, in the main, by a loss of our shared sense of reality, seemed perfectly in tune with other endgames being played around that time, most notably—coming as it did after the death of the author, the demise of the modern subject, and the eclipse of our so-called "master narratives" (the "end of history" prophesied by political scientist Francis Fukuyama after the end of the Cold War). "The twilight of the real"—it sure sounded on point, poignantly capturing some of the primary concerns at large at the time in both art and visual culture. Of course, by the time I had finished writing my thesis, another book had appeared with the no less seductive title *The Return of the Real*, written by Hal Foster, one of the leading theorists, ironically, of the postmodern moment in art. In a nutshell, Foster posited, "After the paradigm of art-as-text in the 1970s and art-as-simulacrum in the 1980s, we are witness to a 'return of the real'—of art and theory that seek to be grounded in actual bodies and social sites." Looking back at some of the period's seminal exhibitions, Foster seems to have been on to something: ambitious shows such as "Féminimasculin" (1995), "L'informe" (1996), "Face à l'histoire" (1996), and the most important and meaningful of all, documenta X (1997), retrospectively appear tellingly united in their attachment to the materiality of history—bodies, matter and stuff—primordial vestiges of the kind of "real" left for dead only a handful of years before: once repressed, now resurgent. Indeed, Foster's "return of the real" partly played out in the refreshingly literal terms of a return of a very particular kind of repression, most viscerally so in art's renewed engagement with the sordid facts of bodily reality, one aspect of that bodily real in particular:

"In the early 1990s this defiance […] was manifested in a general flaunting of shit (or shit substitute: the real thing was rarely found). Of course, Freud understood the disposition to order essential to civilization as a reaction against anal eroticism, and in Civilization and its Discontents he imagined an origin myth involving a related repression that turns on the erection of man from all fours to two feet. With this change in posture, according to Freud, came a revolution in sense: smell was degraded and sight privileged, the anal repressed and the genital pronounced. […] In this light the shit movement in contemporary art may intend a symbolic reversal of this first step into civilization, of the repression of the anal and the olfactory. As such it may also intend a symbolic reversal of the phallic visuality of the erect body as the primary model

of traditional painting and sculpture—the human figure as both the subject and frame of representation in Western art. This double defiance of visual sublimation and vertical form is a strong subcurrent in twentieth-century art, and it is sometimes expressed in a flaunting of anal eroticism." [1]

Peristaltically put: the mid-nineties return of the real was spearheaded, in part, by the "shit movement" in contemporary art.

•

The shit movement in contemporary art must be understood against the backdrop of a wide-ranging sweep of interlocking intuitions and impulses conditioned by the experience of modernism as a moment in cultural history presumably obsessed with intellectual hygiene and moral purity, cleanliness and containment, spotless white cubes, and tightly disciplined ("tight-assed") modes of production. If, according to Clement Greenberg and his puritanical evangelists, the process of modernization in art (i.e. art's becoming "modern") was to be conceived as a process of *purging*

first and foremost—a purification of everything that appears both external and extraneous to the modernist understanding of art—the result was to be a culture of constipation, inevitably calling for ever more radical laxatives. The *non du père* undergirding modernism's ever more anxiously guarded "order of things" inevitably invited ever more violent, visceral critiques, culminating, ultimately, in the return of that which was deemed most taboo and obscene, abject and repulsive—let us call it the *dialectic of the turd* or the *polemic of the poop*. Having spent years, decades even, in stressful, ignoble hiding, sometime in the mid-1990s the brown undercurrent of modernism—its properly critical intestinal edge, so to speak—finally broke into the mainstream of our artistic imagination, resulting in a veritable riot of so-called "abject art" practices only too willing to mess about with excrement, feces, and urine, or menstrual blood, sperm, spit, and other types of bodily waste— the proverbial oil, marble and bronze of the post-postmodern era. Enter the likes of Vito Acconci, Wim Delvoye, Gilbert & George, Mike Kelley, Jeff Koons, John Latham, Paul McCarthy,

Chris Ofili, Carole Schneemann, Andres Serrano, Kiki Smith, Andy Warhol, and (*really* taking shit to the next level) Gelatin of course. [2]

Needless to say, our monolithic notion of a modernist regime obsessed with the compulsive specters of intellectual hygiene and antiseptic form is something of a caricature in turn of course, obscuring a rather more heterogeneous, promiscuous reality. There are obvious historical precedents to the "shit movement" in contemporary art to be found in the work of Marcel Duchamp, for instance, as well as (admittedly the most usual of suspects) that of Piero Manzoni—it is with the latter's well-known *Merde d'artiste* (1960) that the oldest of all truly creative bodily functions is finally let through the front door of modern art history: no more defecating in the dark—a gratifying change from the backdoor delivery of old. (Think of certain gargoyles adorning gothic cathedrals well out of unaided sight, or certain medieval illuminations, or the frenetic, microscopic confusion of a Bosch apocalypse.) Now it is of course in the relationship between Duchamp and Man-

---

1   Hal Foster, *The Return of the Real*, Cambridge: MIT Press, 1996, p. 160.
2   Most of Foster's examples of shit art date back to the early nineties—the time, incidentally, of Gelatin's founding.

zoni and the historical continuum leading from Dada to Neo-Dada, that an added emancipatory move was made in the gradual *desexualization* of the anal event. It is really only with Manzoni that shit, at long last, is finally allowed to be just that—*shit*—and that the shit movement in contemporary art could be said to have come into its own—meaning, primarily, free from the oppressive weight of *gender*, of gendering and its politics. It should be noted here, in this regard, that in his essay on the shit movement in contemporary art, Foster's focus on the work of artists such as Mike Kelley, Paul McCarthy, and Kiki Smith, inevitably yokes the scatological motif back together with the load of gender: Kiki Smith invariably presents the brown streak of abjection in the context of sexual difference (in that the reddish-brown smear always belongs to the female body) while both Mike Kelley's and Paul McCarthy's ostentatious fecal display and "general flaunting of shit" is nearly always linked with infantile, and therefore transgressive, forms of abject sexuality. In these works, the anus remains an agent of difference rather than the seat of sameness—an egalitarian promise perhaps only first fully realized in the work of Gelatin, who allow the turd to address us, at long last, as the irreducible piece

of shit it really is, and as nothing else: a true tour-de-force, obviously, in this most oversexed of all eras. Indeed, it is perhaps precisely by desexualizing and "un-gendering" the excremental event and scatological motif in art that Gelatin's work acquires something of a political charge—away from the identitarian minefield where the sun doesn't shine—towards our (not his, not hers) bodies' genderless output and away from the solipsistic, petty-bourgeois cult of sexual difference and gender assignment to something a little more unifying—the brown bedrock of collective, public, social feeling as opposed to mere private experience. For the more art relegates itself to the phantasmal privacy of the bedroom, the more sorely we feel its retreat from public life. The more autobiographic its motifs and fetishes, the greater we miss its meaning in the civic realm of shared experience. No matter how subversive the spectacle of its many colorful transgressions may appear to us, the oversexed, polyamorous art of our time does not, in the end, pose any real threat to the status quo: its concerns are too private for so common a cause. This, in a political sense, may well be where the roots of the privatization of the anal event in history lie. Perhaps the annexation of the anus by the

forces of adult sexuality coincided with that historic juncture in the time when the communal village loo of old saw itself partitioned in a proliferation of privacies: the first in a long series of assaults on the public sphere that continue, on a much more cerebral and sublimated plane, to this day and in which modern art, with its relentless drive towards sexualization and its incessant worship of all things personal and private, has evidently played a significant role: art is the realm of the "I" par excellence, no longer a world of "we."

Isn't the essence of the toilet contained, in a way, in the mere fact that *we all have to go to it*? ("Even the pope..." "Even the queen..." "Even Elvis…") Isn't the shit we deposit in the toilet the ultimate equalizer (the bodily definition of Bataille's fabled base materialism) and therefore the curse of all identity-inebriated, distinction-obsessed, differentiating "theory"? In going back to the toilet, we return to the real—*together*. Let us think of the john, the loo or latrine—the crapper, privy, shitter, golden stool of relief—as an oracle of sorts, speaking shit's truth to power: a reminder of humankind's union in *matter*.

Critique of Cynical Reason

Peter Sloterdijk

CHAPTER 6

CONCERNING THE PSYCHOSOMATICS OF THE ZEITGEIST

Arses

The arse seems doomed to spend its life in the dark, as the beggar among body Parts. It is the real idiot of the family. However, it would be a wonder if this black sheep of the body did not have its own opinion about everything that takes place in higher regions, similar to the declassed who often cast the most sober gaze on People in the upper strata. If the head were to enter into conversation just once. With its antipode, the latter would first stick out its tongue, if it had one. As in the enlightenment film of the *Rote Grütze, Was heisst hier Liebe* (What do you mean by love?), the arse would say to the higher spheres: I find that our relationship is shitty.

The arse is the plebeian, the grass-roots democrat, and the cosmopolitan among the parts of the body—in a word, the elementary kynical organ. It provides the solid materialist basis. It is at home on toilets all over the world. The International of Arses is the only worldwide organization that has no statutes, ideology, or dues. Its solidarity cannot be shaken. The arse crosses all borders playfully, unlike the head, to which borders and possessions mean a lot. Without any objection, it squats on this or that chair. To an unspoiled arse, the difference between a throne and a kitchen stool, a bench and a Holy Chair is not particularly impressive. Now and again, it can also sit on the ground; the only thing it dislikes is standing when it is tired. This proclivity for the elementary and the fundamental predisposes the arse especially to philosophy. It probably registers the nuances, but it would not think of making a fuss like vain heads do when they knock themselves bloody over the occupation of seats. It never loses sight of what really underlies it: the firm ground. In an erotic sense, too, the arse often shows itself to be both sensitive and superior. It does not pretend to be choosier than is necessary. Even then, it is the one that easily raises itself above imagined borders and exclusivities. When the famous Arletty was accused of having had sexual relations with members of the German occupation forces, her answer is said to have been: "My heart is French, but my backside is international." As representative of the kynical principle per se (able to survive anywhere, reduction to the essentials), the arse can hardly be brought under government control, although it cannot be denied that many an arsehole has given off nationalistic tones.

Often beaten, kicked, and pinched, the arse has a worldview from below: plebeian, popular, realistic. Millennia of bad treatment have not passed over it without leaving a mark. They have trained it to be a materialist, albeit one with a dialectical tendency, which assumes that things are shitty but not hopeless. Nothing can cause as much bitterness as the feeling of not being welcome. Only the undertone of fascination that can be heard through so much maltreatment gives the oppressed a secret feeling of power. Something about which silence is so stubbornly maintained, even though it cannot be evaded, must have a great power over the spirits. The best energies are often hidden behind the strongest swear words. It is as if all the maltreated backsides are waiting for their hour of revenge in the near future, when everything will again be falling flat on its arse. The feeling for time is generally one of the special strengths of arses, for very early on they develop a feeling for what has to be done immediately, for what can be postponed, and for what a well-padded behind can wait out patiently until doomsday. That is really a political art that today is called timing and that has its roots in a praxis even children's arses learn, namely, to perform what has to be at the right time, not too early and not too late.

The arse triumphs secretly, conscious that without it nothing works. Being there precedes being such and such; first existence, then qualities; first reality, then good and evil, above and below. Thus arses are, in addition to their dialectical-materialist inclinations, also the first existentialists. They practice the existential dialectic in advance: Should one decide in favor of what has to be in any case, or does one choose to revolt against the unavoidable? Even those who decide to let things take their course have decided, as Sartre says, not to decide. Freedom surrenders to necessity. One can, however, also decide against it—not, of course, against the fact that one must, but against the fact that the must can do anything at all with one. One can struggle against it and hold back what has to be; then one becomes, following Camus,

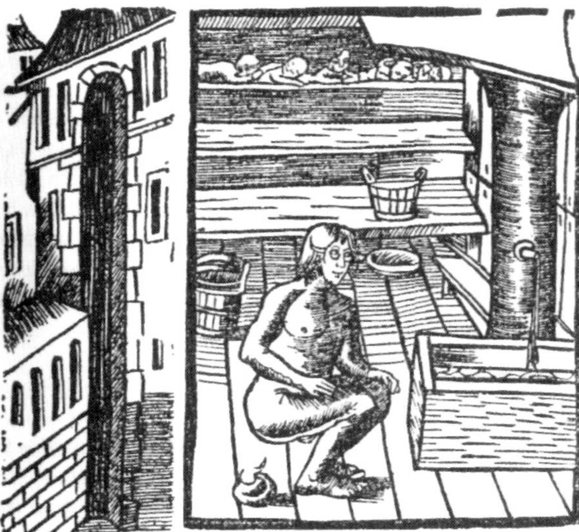

… how Eulenspiegel shat in a bathroom in Hannover and claimed it was a house of purity. Woodcut illustration from a popular book, 1515.

the person in revolt. Nobody must must, says Lessing's Nathan, and the popular saying adds: Dying and shitting are the only things one must do. That remains the kynical a priori. The arse is thus, of all bodily organs, the one closest to the dialectical relation of freedom and necessity. It is no accident that psychoanalysis—a thoroughly kynically inspired discipline—devotes subtle investigations to it and names a fundamental anthropological stage, the anal phase, after the experiences and vicissitudes of the arse. Its themes are Can and Cannot, Must and Must not, Have and Hold Back. The Principle of achievement is contained in it. To understand the arse would be therefore the best preparatory study for philosophy, the somatic propaedeutic. How many constipated theories we would be spared! Again we meet up with Diogenes. He was the first European philosopher who, instead of employing a lot of words in the Athenian market, performed his urgent business. *Naturalia non sunt turpia*. In nature, he says, we find nothing about which we would have to be ashamed. Real bestiality and perverted spirits are found where the arrogance of morality and the imbroglio of culture begin. The heads, however, did not want to recognize that this was an early climax of reason, a moment in which philosophy had found a balance with the principle of nature. For a moment, it was beyond good and evil and beyond turning up its nose. Respectable thinkers, on the other hand insist on their view; according to them, it can only have been a joke or a provocative dirty trick. They refuse to conjecture that there could be a truth-producing meaning in such a manifestation.

Shit, Refuse

Here we come to the whole of the matter. As children of an anal culture, wc all have a more or less disturbed relation to our own shit. The splitting off of our consciousness from our own shit is the deepest training in order; it tells us what must happen privately and under wraps. The relation that is drummed into people with regard to their own excretions provides the model for their behavior with all sorts of refuse in their lives. Hitherto, refuse was systematically ignored. Only under the sign of modern ecological thinking do we find ourselves forced to become conscious again of our refuse. High theory discovers the category "shit"; a new stage of the philosophy of nature thereby comes due, a critique of the human being as a hyperproductive shit-accumulating industry-animal. Diogenes is the only Western philosopher who we know consciously and publicly performed his animal business, and there are reasons to interpret this as a component of a pantomimic theory. It hints at a consciousness of nature that assigns positive values to the animal side of human beings and does not allow any dissociation of what is low or embarrassing. Those who do not want to admit that they produce refuse and that they cannot choose to do anything else risk suffocating one day in their own shit. Everything suggests that Diogenes of Sinope should be admitted to the Ancestral Gallery of Ecological Consciousness. The grand act of ecology in the history of ideas that will have an impact as far as philosophy, ethics, and Politics are concerned will be to transform the phenomenon of refuse into a "high" theme. From now on it is no longer an onerous secondary phenomenon but is recognized as a basic principle. With this, the last hidden positions of idealism and dualism are really broken down. Shit has to be encountered in another way. It is now necessary to rethink the usefulness of the unuseful, the productivity of unproductive, philosophically speaking: to unlock the positivity of the negative and to recognize our responsibility also for what is unintended. Kynical philosophers are those who do not get nauseated. In this they are related to children, who do not yet know anything about the negativity of their excrement.

Translation by Michael Eldred

Copyright © 1987 by the University of Minnesota

Originally published as *Kritik der zynischen Vernunft*, 2 vols.

Copyright © 1983 by Suhrkamp Verlag, Frankfurt am Main

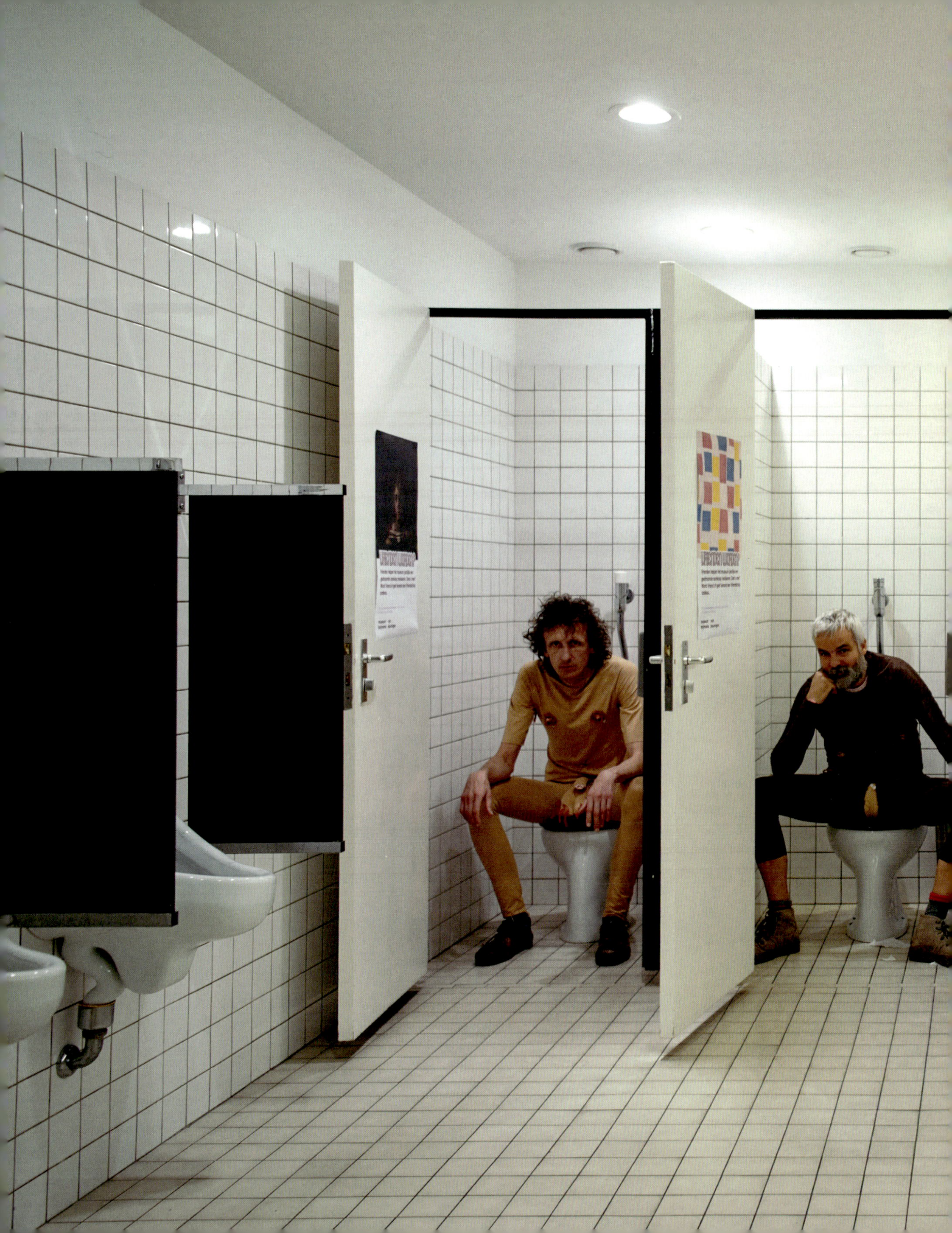

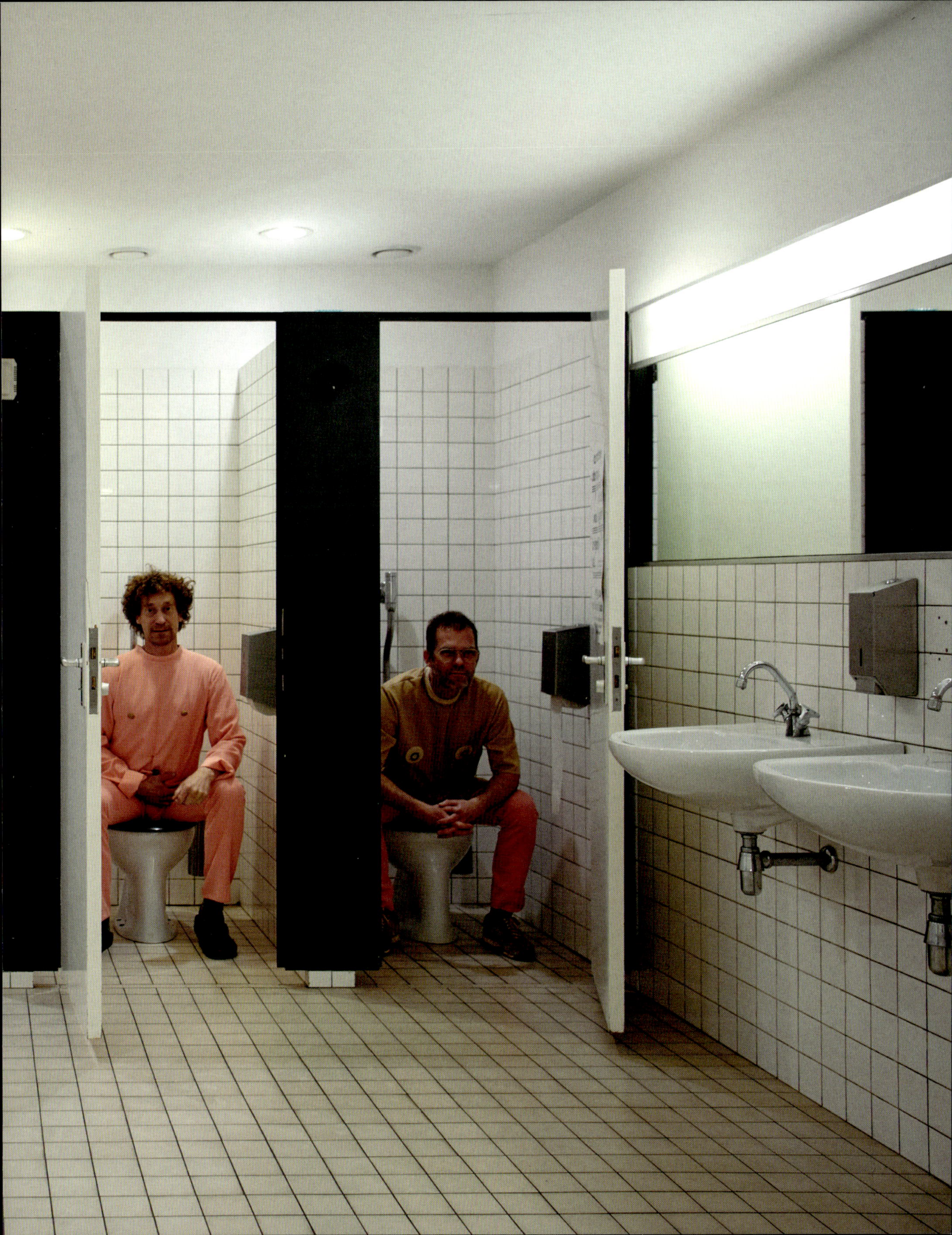

This book is published on the occasion of the exhibition "Gelatin: Vorm – Fellows – Attitude" Museum Boijmans Van Beuningen, Rotterdam May 19 to August 12, 2018.

Director: Sjarel Ex
Curator: Francesco Stocchi
Production: Lotte van Diggelen

Gelatin *with:*
Christoph Harringer, Anna Schwarz, Bert Löschner,
Manuel Scheiwiller, Helmut Heiss, Olga Wukounig,
Scott Clifford Evans, Martina Noskova,
Kolbeinn Hugi Höskuldsson, Olivia Reither,
Tom Van Camp, Iris Schuttevaar, Jason Schmidt,
Manó Dániel Szöllösi, Lili Ullrich, Mario Gamser,
Jackie Lee, Mahyar, Josefine Reither, Roland Klima,
Sue van Geijn, Gerhard Riml, Familie Levinitschnig,
Georg Holzmann, Jan Weiler and the team Boijmans.

Translations:
Tristam Bruce, Lynn Richards

Supported by:
Phileas
Legero United
Bundeskanzleramt Österreich
Galleria Massimo De Carlo
Galerie Perrotin
Tim Van Laere Gallery
Galerie Meyer Kainer
Claytec
Schuyler Maehl

2018 © Gelatin, authors and
Verlag der Buchhandlung Walther König

Editor:
Museum Boijmans Van Beuningen
Museumpark 18-20
3015 CX Rotterdam, The Netherlands
Tel: +31 (0) 10 44 19 400
www.boijmans.nl

Design: Aki Namba

Photos by:
Lotte Stekelenburg for Museum Boijmans Van Beuningen
Jason Schmidt, Georg Holzmann, Markus Tretter, Knut Klaßen

Published by / Distribution:
Buchhandlung Walther König
Ehrenstr. 4
D - 50672 Köln
Fon +49 (0) 221 / 20 59 6 53
verlag@buchhandlung-walther-koenig.de

The German Library catalogs this publication
in the German National Bibliography;
detailed bibliographic information can be found
on the Internet website:
http://dnb.d-nb.de

Printed in Austria

ISBN 978-3-96098-432-0